IN YOUR GARDEN AGAIN

Published by
OXENWOOD PRESS LTD 1998

an imprint of Cover to Cover Cassettes Ltd
P.O. Box 112, Marlborough, Wiltshire SN8 3UG

First published by
MICHAEL JOSEPH LTD 1953

IN YOUR GARDEN AGAIN
Text copyright © Vita Sackville-West 1955
Illustrations copyright © Oxenwood Press 1998

A CIP catalogue record for this book is available
from the British Library

ISBN 0–9527801 9

IN YOUR GARDEN AGAIN is also available as Cover to Cover
audio cassettes

In Your Garden Again *Spring and Summer* ISBN: 18859 805 7
In Your Garden Again *Autumn and Winter* ISBN: 1 85549 806 5

Printed and bound in Great Britain by
Butler & Tanner Ltd, Frome and London

Achilles.

V. SACKVILLE-WEST

In Your Garden Again

Oxenwood Press

Foreword

THIS is a second collection of articles contributed on Sundays to *The Observer*, covering the dates between February 18, 1951, and March 8, 1953. As in the previous volume, the months have been grouped together irrespective of the year in which the articles appeared. I am afraid this system may have the effect of bringing some rather repetitive remarks too close together, but on the whole it seemed the best system to adopt, and I would ask readers to remember that these articles in their original form were spaced seasonally at weekly intervals over two years.

As in the previous volume, I have added many names and addresses of nurserymen from whom the plants mentioned may be obtained. There is also an appendix of names and addresses at the end. There is also an index.

With great regret, I learn that Mr. Ralph Cusack, for reasons of health, is obliged to give up his nursery. I have, however, left his name wherever it occurs, in the hope that his retirement may be delayed, or that some successor may carry on.

I would again like to thank *The Observer* for their courtesy in allowing me to reprint these articles in book form.

V. S.-W.

Sissinghurst Castle,
Cranbrook,
Kent.

Contents

Botanical Illustrations
by Frederick W. Smith

Index of Plants

January

January 6, 1952

IT often happens that an old, rough hedge occurs somewhere in a garden; a hedge which presents a problem.
Too heavy a job to grub out, too expensive to replace,
and giving no pleasure to the eye, being composed of a
thorny rubbishy mixture, usefully dense but unaesthetic.
It is possible to add some interest and colour by planting
climbers to ramble along and over this sort of inherited
relic.

Obviously, these climbers will have to be tough. They
will have a great deal of competition to put up with, a
starved root-run, a spiteful host, and a slash of ungentle
trimming in the autumn, probably administered by a
countryman with a billhook and a pair of shears. Yet if
you reflect on the survival of such things as the wild
honeysuckle and the wild clematis, Old Man's Beard or
Traveller's Joy, in precisely those conditions, you will see
that it should not be impossible to devise a collection of
slightly more sophisticated trailers to transform the old
hedge from a dull thing into a thing garlanded, here and
there, with some streaks of beauty.

A rough hedge, as a matter of fact, offers a real opportunity to the enterprising gardener. We should take a hint
from Nature, and plant such things as normally thrive in
such unkind circumstances. The wild honeysuckle suggests
the garden varieties of climbing (as opposed to shrubby)
honeysuckles; the wild clematis suggests the more tenacious

of the garden sorts. I can imagine *Clematis montana*, either the white or the pink, throwing itself like a cloak over the top of the hedge; a single plant of this should cover an area of fifteen feet within a very few years. *Clematis flammula*, white and sweet-scented, should do as well, and should not too greatly resent being hacked about when the time comes for the autumnal brishing. Then, remembering how the wild dog-rose flourishes, we should try some rambling roses of the Wichuriana type, Alberic Barbier, creamy; Albertine, a coppery pink; François Juranville, pink-and-tea. One might also try a wistaria. It would be amusing to see some long tassels of wistaria dangling from amongst the common quick or thorn.

I can imagine also our disgraced and discarded old friend, the Virginia creeper, looking very fine in this novel position, or indeed any of the ornamental vines which colour well, if you can ensure that the hedge is not trimmed too early. *Celastrus articulatus* (or *orbiculatus*) with golden berries splitting open to reveal orange seed-pods, would perhaps be even more satisfactory growing horizontally than up a tree or over a shed, and it would certainly be easier to pick the berries.

January 13, 1952

As a rule I try to be practical in these articles, recommending only such plants as can be grown with some hope of success by the amateur gardener having no advantage of glass or any similar luxury. For once, however, I would like to introduce a climber which does demand shelter from frost, although it may stand out of doors in its pot happily throughout the summer, and, failing a greenhouse, could be safely preserved in a warm room in winter. To do this, you would have to keep it within reasonable bounds by training it round some hoops of sticks, when it makes the most charming pot-plant imaginable. It is so pretty, it

flowers so continuously, and smells so deliciously sweet, that
it justifies all this extra trouble.

Its name is *Jasminum polyanthum*, a fairly recent introduction from China where I believe it was discovered by
Major Lawrence Johnston, that great gardener and creator
of the garden at Hidcote. Not very well known here as
yet, it may be obtained for the modest sum of 5s. 6d., and
as it strikes very readily from cuttings a home-grown stock
may be raised within a very short time if wanted. To look
at, it resembles the familiar white summer-flowering
jasmine, *officinale*, but the flowers are larger, the scent
twenty times as powerful, and the rosy, pointed buds are
so pretty among the dark green leaves as to be like little
jewels in themselves. I have a sprig six inches long on my
table, today in January, carrying twenty-two buds, so its
name *polyanthum*, meaning many-flowered, is manifestly
well deserved. On the parent plant, now standing in an
unheated glass lean-to, a few flowers are already open, a
real boon in January. I hope I have said enough to stir
temptation.

In the milder counties it could, of course, be grown out
of doors, and I have in fact seen a magnificent specimen
reaching as high as the eaves of the house in Major Stern's
famous garden, Highdown, near Goring-on-Sea, in Sussex.
Here it has the wall to protect it from the north wind, and
the sea-air which always means less frost. In Devon or
Cornwall, or in some sheltered parts of Somerset, Dorset,
and Wales, I imagine that it would grow exuberantly and
to a great height. Like all such twining things, it tends
to get into a tangle, which, as all gardeners know to their
cost, leads to a lot of dead wood in the centre and is plaguy
to control. The best way of thwarting this airless, lightless
jungle is to train some strong shoots sideways, away from
the main stem; otherwise we shall find ourselves with a task
like unravelling several milesworth of mad hanks of string.

B

For those whose interest I may have caught by this mention of the Chinese jasmine, I might end by a reference to the Cape jasmine, *J. angulare*, which is said to be even more fragrant. Both these jasmines may be obtained from Treseders' Nurseries, Truro, Cornwall.

January 20, 1952

Climbers are among the most useful plants in any garden. They take up little ground space, and they can be employed for many purposes: to clothe a boring fence, to scramble over a dead tree, to frame an archway, to drape a wall, to disguise a shed, or to climb lightly into a pergola. They demand comparatively little attention, once they have taken hold of their support, maybe a yearly pruning or a kindly rescue if they have come adrift in a gale.

The clematis is perhaps as popular as any, despite its distressing addiction to the disease known as *wilt*. Few garden-lovers can resist the splendid mid-summer purple of the Jackmanii hybrids, but there are other forms to choose from, for instance *C. Spooneri*, an ivory-white with curly edges, or *Armandii Snowdrift*, pure white with pointed, evergreen leaves, or, if you prefer a cloud of smoky blue, *Perle d'azur* and *Jouiniana praecox*. If you would like a yellow, with hanging flowers like tiny Chinese lanterns, try *C. tangutica Gravetye variety;* it may not be very showy, but it has its charm when you stand underneath it and look up into its little golden bells.

The enterprising gardener will, however, want to get away from the more obvious climbers, amongst which the clematis must, I suppose, be included. What about *Akebia quinata* and *Akebia trifoliata*, sometimes listed as *A. lobata*? They are not often seen, but they should be. They are both strong growers, semi-evergreen, with shamrock-like leaves and curiously coloured flowers. The flowers of *A. trifoliata* are brown, and the flowers of *A. quinata* are

of a dusty violet, which might best be described by that
neglected adjective, *gridelin*. Both kinds are hardy, and
in a mild climate or after a hot sunny summer will produce
fruits the size of a duck's egg, if you will imagine a duck's
egg in plum-colour, with a plum's beautiful bloom before
it has got rubbed off in the marketing. These fruits have
the advantage that their seeds will germinate 100 per cent
if you sow them in a pot; at any rate, that has been my
experience.

The Akebias will grow tall if you let them, but if you
want something which will never exceed 8 to 10 feet let
me recommend *Actinidia Kolomitka* as a plant to set against
a wall facing east or west. The small white flowers are
insignificant and may be disregarded; the beauty lies in
the leaves, which are triple-coloured, green and pink and
white, so gay and decorative and unusual as to provoke
friends and visitors into asking what it is.

January 27, 1952

I wrote about climbers last week, but there were many
I had no space to mention. I wanted to put in a good word
for the Passion flower, *Passiflora coerulea*, which is hardier
than sometimes supposed, springing up from its roots again
yearly, even if it has been cut down to the ground by
frost and has apparently given up all attempt to live. Its
strangely constructed flowers are not very effective at a
distance, but marvellous to look into, with the nails and
the crown of thorns from which it derives its name. It
should be grown against a warm wall, though even in so
favoured a situation I fear it is unlikely to produce its
orange fruits in this country.* There is a white variety

* I must go back on this remark. Plants on two cottages near where
I live, in Kent, produce a truly heavy crop of fruits. I could not think
what they were till I stopped to investigate. The curious thing is that
both plants are facing due east, and can scarcely receive any sun at all.
See also February 10, 1952.

called Constance Elliott. I prefer the pale blue one myself;
but each to his own taste.

Then the Bignonias. I know that I have often mentioned
them in these articles, but they are so showy and so
decorative that I must insist once again. Their big orange
red trumpets make a noise like a brass band in the summer
garden. They are things with a rather complicated botanical
history, often changing their names. *Bignonia grandiflora*
is now known as *Campsis grandiflora* (it went through
a phase of calling itself Tecoma) and *Bignonia radicans* is
now *Campsis radicans*. The best variety of it is *Mme Galen*;
and as it has rather smaller flowers than *grandiflora*, a
friend of mine calls it Little-nonia, a poor joke that will
not appeal to serious gardeners, but may be helpful to the
amateurs who wish to remember the difference.

They all want a sunny wall, and should be pruned back
like a vine, that is, cut right hard back to a second 'eye'
or bud, during the dormant season between November and
January. Like a vine, again, they will strike from cuttings
taken at an eye and pushed firmly into sandy soil.

Berberidopsis corallina, from Chile, whose second name
describes the colour of its flowers, has the advantage of
being evergreen and of not objecting to a shady wall, where
its beautiful racemes will hang in a rich glow. I think this
range of colours, orange or coral or red, gains in splendour
from a shadowy place. *Berberidopsis* has, however, two
disadvantages: it does not like any lime in the soil, and its
hardiness is not above reproach. Given a sheltered corner,
it should survive most winters, especially in the south or
west.

January 4, 1953

It has been asserted that, since we admire flowers chiefly
because they are not green, it is natural that green flowers
should fail to arouse much enthusiasm. If that allegation

be true, then our two native hellebores must be ruled out.
But I dispute it. The green rose, *R. viridiflora*, gives me
much amusement; and I have always longed to come
across a plant of the green primrose. I like green flowers,
especially when they are of a bright apple-green as in
Helleborus viridis, commonly called Bear's Foot, or in
Helleborus foetidus, the Setterwort, even more commonly
and certainly more rudely called the Stinking hellebore,
found in beechwoods in company of *Daphne Laureola* and
the Dog's Mercury spurge. Besides, I like any plant that
will surprise me out of doors with flowers in January or
February.

Perhaps it may soften prejudiced hearts if I add that the
hellebores belong to the same botanical family as the
buttercups, the *Ranunculaceae*. Few of the English—a most
sentimental race—can resist the appeal of the buttercup
and those gold-besprent meadows of childhood, and the
Kingcups growing along the banks of a stream.

Our two native hellebores are becoming rare now, so
if you have the luck to find them growing wild in the
chalky soil of the South Downland country, please do not
dig them up, but make a note to order plants or seeds
from a nurseryman* or seedsman. Seeds germinate quickly
when they are freshly harvested. It is said that ants
distribute them in Nature: but as we cannot rely on an
obliging ant-heap it is better to buy a packet of fresh seed
for ninepence and sow it at once in a seed box and prick
out the plantlings later in the usual way.

I will not contend that either of our two natives is as
handsome a plant as the Corsican cousin, *Helleborus corsicus*,
so strong and stout that its leaves alone have an architectural
quality in the same sense as the Acanthus has an architectural or sculptural quality, quite apart from the beauty

* Mr. W. Th. Ingwersen has plants; address on p. 176. Messrs.
Thompson & Morgan have seeds. Address on p. 176.

and value of the flowers. But I do contend that our two
natives are worth adding to any collection of the hellebores.
They are humble, and make few demands. They will put
up with a considerable amount of shade, and they do not
mind lime, in fact they like it, two considerations that
ought to appeal to people with difficult patches in their
gardens.

Do not be alarmed if *H. viridis* dies away in autumn;
it is not dead, it is resting, and will revive. *H. foetidus*,
on the contrary, is evergreen.

January 11, 1953

I went to a Christmas party given by a neighbour of
mine, a member of a great hereditary firm of seedsmen,
almost feudal in their family tradition. His baptismal name,
most appropriate to the season, was Noël. All the things
appertaining to a cocktail party were standing about, on
tables; but the thing that instantly caught my eye was a
pot-plant of cyclamen I had not seen for years.

Delicate in its quality, subtle in its scent, which resembles
the scent of wood-violets, it stood there in a corner by
itself, looking so modest and Jane-Austen-like among its
far grander companions. It had a freshness and an inno-
cence about it, a sort of adolescent look, rather frightened
at finding itself in company of orchids and choice azaleas
and glasses filled with champagne cocktails.

It was the little Persian cyclamen, in its original size
before it had got 'improved' by nurserymen and swollen
into its present inflated form. May I here make a protest
against the fashion for exaggerating the size of flowers?
Bigger, but not thereby better. Those vast begonias; those
tree-trunk delphiniums; those mops of chrysanthemums,
all those things called *giganteum*—does anyone really like
them, except the growers who get the gold medals?

Ah, no, I thought, looking at the little Persian cyclamen,

white, pink-tipped, shy, unobtrusive, demure; this is the
way I like my flowers to be; not puffed up as though by
a pair of bellows; not shouting for praise from gaping
admirers.

I have never seen it growing wild in Persia. Apparently
it grows wild also in Cyprus and in Rhodes.

I wish it were easier to obtain.* You can buy or be
given the big cyclamen at any florist's shop, and I am not
saying anything against them. They are a wonderful
stand-by at this time of the year, and with due care their
corms should last year after year, reviving again in July
or August to start on their job of flowering once more
before next Christmas. But handsome though they are,
these big Christmas-present cyclamen, they do not possess
the Tom-tit, Jenny-wren, leveret-eared character of the
little Persian.

January 18, 1953

Not for the first time I find myself at a loss to know
what to write about. January is a dead season, when one
cannot get out to do anything active in the garden, so one
is reduced to studying catalogues under the lamp and
thereby being induced to order far more plants or seeds
than one ought to.

I have ordered a summer-flowering tamarisk, *Tamarix
pentandra*. This will flower in August, I hope, during that
month when flowering shrubs are few. We do not grow
the tamarisks enough; they are so graceful, so light and
buoyant, so feathery, so pretty when smothered in their
rose-pink flower. The earlier-flowering one is *Tamarix
tetrandra*; it comes out in April to May.

The seed catalogues are my undoing. I have grown wise,
after many years of gardening, and no longer order recklessly from wildly alluring descriptions which make every

* Small plants can be got from Messrs. Blackmore & Langdon, Bath.

annual sound easy to grow and as brilliant as a film star.
I now know that gardening is not like that. Yet I can still
be decoyed into ordering some packets of the Roggli pansies
and the Chabaud carnations, having learnt from experience
how good and repaying they are. The pansies, if sown in
March under glass, will scarcely flower this summer, or
at any rate not until September, but twelve months later
they should have made fine clumps which will start
flowering in May and should continue without remission
until the first autumn frosts. The annual carnations, however, if sown in February under glass (a seed box in a
frame or under a hand-light) should fill bare patches
during the ensuing summer and are as pretty and scented
as anyone could desire. They can be had in self-colours,
or flaked and striped like the pinks in old flower-paintings;
with their old-fashionable look they associate perfectly with
the Damask and Gallica and Cabbage roses.

'Carnation' is perhaps a misleading term, since to most
people, myself included, carnation suggests a greenhouse
plant of the Malmaison type; an expensive buttonhole for
a dandy at Ascot or Lord's. The Chabaud carnations are
more like what we think of as our grandmother's pinks.

Please make a point of getting the two strains I have
recommended: the Roggli pansies, and the Chabaud carnations, whether annual or perennial. They are by far the
best I know and the seeds may be obtained from Mr. George
Roberts, Davington, Faversham, Kent.

January 25, 1953

There are certain roses whose charm lies in their foliage
as much as in their flowers. They are the roses whose
foliage one can describe only by calling it fern-like; and
by that I do not mean the ferns of woodland or damp
places, but the so-called Maidenhair fern which used to
be grown in company of smilax for the decoration of dinner

tables at public banquets, and perhaps, for all I know, still is.

First among these tiny-leaved roses I would put *Rosa Farreri persetosa*, otherwise known as the Threepenny-bit rose. It could not be better named, for its bright pink flower is no larger than the old silver thrup'ny bit we seldom have in our pockets or purses now, since it has been replaced by a solid twelve-sided coin of a baser metal. I am told that in Burma it is known as the four-anna bit rose. The Thrup'ny-bit rose is a rare darling, a tiny treasure; not tiny as to growth, for it will go up to six or seven feet high; but tiny as to its leaves and its flock of miniature flowers in early summer. It comes from the South Kansu province of China, growing wild in the Ta-tung Alps, where it was found by Reginald Farrer in 1914. It is perfectly hardy, and renews its prettiness in autumn with small red fruits and colouring leaves.*

Other small-leaved roses, all of which will make a big loose shrubby bush, are *Hugonis* and *Cantabridgensis*, smothered with butter-yellow flowers in May; *Rosa primula*, yellow; *Rosa rubrifolia*, whose beauty lies chiefly in the contrast between the grey-green leaves and stems the colour of a Victoria plum; *Rosa Willmottiae*, pale pink, usually the first of all to flower and valuable on that score alone, but with the tiresome fault of making an exaggerated amount of dead twiggy wood armed with real little savages of thorns when one goes to clear it out for its own advantage. *Rosa Omiensis*, white-flowered, has ferocious blood-red thorns, half an inch long, magnificent when the rising or setting sun strikes through them, so take the hint and plant this rose where it will catch the morning or the evening light.

There are other roses which may be chosen for their delicate foliage, their wildly generous growth, and their

* Messrs. T. Hilling stock it.

willingness to fill an otherwise wasted corner. I meant simply to give an indication of what can be found by the intelligent gardener looking through the descriptive catalogues issued by nurserymen who specialize in roses other than the well-known hybrid teas and ramblers. See addresses on p. 177.

May I add, to correct what seems to be a misapprehension on the part of many people, that roses can still safely be planted up to the beginning or middle of March.

February

ONCE I wrote about flowering trees trained along wires in front gardens, and ended up with a hint about rose-hedges to grow along the pavement of a village street. Not necessarily a village, but a small country town, or even a suburb or a new housing estate; anywhere that demands a hedge to divide the front garden from the road.

In a gracious, small and ancient town near where I live, someone has had the imagination to plant just such a hedge of rambler roses. It occupies the whole of his road frontage, about 150 yards I believe, and in the summer months people come from all over the county to see it. I must admit that it is an impressive sight; a blaze of colour; a long, angry, startling streak, as though somebody had taken a red pencil and had scrawled dense red bunches all over a thicket-fence of green. A splendid idea; very effective; but, oh, how crude! I blink on seeing it; and having blinked, I weep. It is not only the virulence of the colour that brings tears to my eyes, but the regret that so fine an idea should not have been more fastidiously carried out.

The hedge is made of *American Pillar*, a rose which, together with *Dorothy Perkins*, should be forever abolished from our gardens. I know this attack on two popular roses will infuriate many people; but if one writes gardening articles one must have the courage of one's opinion. I hate,

hate, hate *American Pillar* and her sweetly pink companion *Perkins*. What would I have planted instead? Well, there is *Goldfinch*, an old rambler, very vigorous, very sweet-scented, and when I say sweet-scented I mean it, for I do try to tell the exact truth in these articles, not to mislead anybody. *Goldfinch* is a darling; she is my pet, my treasure; a mass of scrambled eggs. Then there is *Félicité et Perpétue*, white, flushed pink; and *Madame Plantier*, white, with larger flowers. Or *Albertine*, very strong and free-flowering, a beautiful soft pink that appears to have been dipped in tea; or *François Juranville* who has also fallen into a tea-cup.

February 25, 1951

Is the Winter Aconite too well known to deserve mention? Surely not. We cannot be reminded too often of so dear and early a thing. It started flowering here, in Kent, on January 20th; I made a note in my diary. Then frost came, turning it into tiny crystallized apricots, like the preserved fruits one used once to get given for Christmas. They shone; they sparkled in the frost. Then the frost went, and with the thaw they emerged from their rimy sugar coating into their full, smooth, buttercup yellow on a February day with its suggestion of spring, when the first faint warmth of the sun falls as a surprise upon our naked hands.

I am being strictly correct in comparing the varnished yellow of the Winter Aconite to our common buttercup, for they both belong to the same botanical order of the *Ranunculaceae*.

The proper name of the Winter Aconite is *Eranthis*. *Eranthis hyemalis* is the one usually grown, and should be good enough for anybody. It costs only 2s. 6d. a dozen, but if you want a superior variety you can order *E. Tubergeni*, more expensive, at 10s. 6d. or 12s. 6d. a dozen. I daresay this would be worth trying. Personally I am very well satisfied with the smudge of gold given me by *hyemalis* (meaning, of winter). It has the great advantage of flourishing almost anywhere, in shade or sun, under trees or in the open, and also of producing a generous mustard-and-cress-like crop of self-sown seedlings which you can lift and transplant. It is better to do this than to lift the older plants, for it is one of those home-lovers that likes to stay put, and, indeed, will give of its best only when it has had a couple of years to become established. So do not get impatient with it at first. Give it time.

There are many small early things one could happily associate with it; in fact, I can imagine, and intend to plant, a winter corner, stuffed with little companions all giving their nursery party at the same time: *Narcissus minimus* and *Narcissus nanus*; the bright blue thimbles of the earliest grape hyacinth, *Muscari azureus*; the delicate spring crocus *Tomasinianus*, who sows himself everywhere, scores of little Thomases all over the place . . . but I must desist.

February 3, 1952

It suddenly occurred to me that I had never written about pergolas in this column nor am I quite sure that pergolas are altogether suitable for this country. They drip. Moreover, they are all too often used as a support for the less desirable kinds of rambler rose and their usefulness as a framework for more interesting climbers is often overlooked. Practically all the flowering climbers look fine thus seen overhead, and to them may be added the many sorts of ornamental vine, including the hardy fruiting vines, for what could be prettier than bunches of little grapes dangling, either green or black?

Even the people who prefer to stick exclusively to roses have a wide choice of very beautiful and vigorous varieties.

There are old favourites amongst them: *Gloire de Dijon,
Lady Hillingdon, Mme Alfred Carrière, William Allen
Richardson*; but there are also some loose, huge single or
semi-double flowerers: *Allen Chandler*, a blaze of red with
golden centres; *Cupid*, a silvery shell-pink; *Emily Gray*,
a butter-yellow with shiny dark leaves and reddish stems;
and the well-known *Mermaid*, flowering late, a delicate
yellow. Many of the favourite hybrid teas may also be had
as climbers: *Crimson Glory, Etoile de Hollande, Ophelia,
Mme Edouard Heriot.* Then there is *Paul's Lemon Pillar*,
one of the most perfectly shaped roses I know, and of so
subtle a colour that one does not know whether to call it
ivory or sulphur or iceberg green. A very rich yellow is
Lawrence Johnston, once known as *Hidcote Yellow*; and
for a mixture of yellow and red, giving an effect of the
most brilliant orange, you have *Réveil Dijonnais*, greatly
resembling the old Austrian Copper, which, in fact, is one
of its parents, only with far larger flowers. Startling when
it first opens, it has the fault of fading into a truly hideous
pinkish mud.

These are only a very few of the substitutes I would
suggest for my old enemies *American Pillar* and *Dorothy
Perkins*.

I get grumbled at from time to time for recommending
roses that don't figure in some rose-growers' catalogues,
so may I refer the reader to some addresses given on
p. 177 of this book?

February 10, 1952

A lady writes to say she has an ugly porch to her house,
and what evergreen climber can she grow to cover it up?
Her hope is to obscure the porch all the year round. No
doubt many people find themselves in a similar predica-
ment, so a note on the subject may be useful. The trouble
is that few climbers, with the exception of ivy, are ever-

green; and that those which are, tend to be only half-hardy. Amongst true evergreen climbers I can think of two honeysuckles, Giraldii and Henryii; one of each, planted either side of the porch, should soon grow up to interwine overhead. But this does not take us very far, and it becomes necessary to look round for some substitutes.

We may find them amongst the tall-growing shrubs which can be treated as a kind of buttress or side-piers, and induced by means of wire to grow horizontally across the top. *Ceanothus rigidus* and *Ceanothus thyrsiflorus* both come to mind, with dark green leaves and powder-blue flowers; reasonably hardy, they will attain a height of twelve to thirty feet respectively. They could not, however, look so tidy as something which could be clipped into shape; and that makes me think of the Sweet Bay, *Laurus nobilis*. You know how sometimes on old country cottages one sees a kind of deep, dense porch, generally cut out of yew or box, giving an air of solidity and mystery to the entrance, which would be especially welcome in a brand-new, perhaps rather insubstantial, dwelling? There is no reason why the Sweet Bay, with its aromatic foliage, should not be used for a similar purpose, to frame and disguise the objectionable porch. It is of fairly rapid growth, and will put up with any amount of shaping. Within a few years it should provide the front door with a dark-green cavern of shelter.

*   *   *

If my correspondent thinks this sounds gloomy, though personally I think that a bit of gloom is of immense value in a garden, as a foil to the bright flowers, she might try planting two of the poplar-like cherries as sentinels either side of her porch. True, they are not evergreen, but their mass of pale pink blossom is a delight of youthfulness in spring. *Prunus Lannesiana erecta* is the name, or Amanogawa, meaning Celestial River, the Japanese equivalent of our Milky Way.

May I thank all those enviable people who have written to say that their Passion flower does produce its fruits in their gardens? Mostly west-country gardens, I may add, though there was one triumphant letter from Hampshire, which is not so very far west.

February 17, 1952

Amongst other seeds for spring sowing I ordered a sixpenny packet of *Mimosa pudica*, the Humble Plant. Most people, including some nurserymen, call it the Sensitive Plant, a name that should be reserved for *Mimosa sensitiva*, which contradictorily, is less sensitive than *M. pudica*. So humble is the Humble Plant, so bashful, that a mere touch of the finger or a puff of breath blown across it will cause it to collapse instantly into a woebegone heap, like the once popular Ally Sloper. One grows it purely for the purpose of amusing the children. The normal child, if not an insufferable prig, thoroughly enjoys being unkind to something; so here is a harmless outlet for this instinct in the human young. Shrieks of delight are evoked, enhanced by the sadistic pleasure of doing it over and over again. 'Let's go back and see if it has sat up yet.' It probably has, for it seems to be endowed with endless patience under such mischievous persecution.

I must admit that I would like to see it in its native home in tropical America, where, I have been told, acres of pigmy forest swoon under the touch of a ruffling breeze. Nominally a perennial there, it is best treated as a half-hardy annual here. This means that we must sow our sixpenny packet in a pot or a pan under glass or on the window-sill of a warm room. By late summer it will have grown up into quite a tall plant about a foot high; and then you may observe that, like most sensitive people, it

Elizabeth   Homer

Marcelhis.

is not only sensitive but prickly. It develops large spiky thorns, but still retains its shivering fright. It then becomes not only an amusement for children but a symbol for many of our friends.

If these joke plants interest you I have several more in mind. For instance, the Burning Bush, *Dictamnus fraxinella* or Dittany, which you can set alight into a blue flame, especially on a warm summer day, without any harm to the plant. The explanation of this apparent miracle is the presence of a volatile oil; but why seek for explanations when you can so easily entertain your young guests?

Seeds of *Mimosa pudica* and of the Burning Bush, *Dictamnus fraxinella* can be bought from Messrs. Thompson & Morgan, Ipswich; but it is better and quicker to get a plant of the Burning Bush at 1s. 9d. from W. Th. Ingwersen, address on p. 176.

February 24, 1952

Last Sunday in this column I was writing about joke plants, but had to stop short. I wanted to go on about the Marvel of Peru, *Mirabilis Jalapa*, familiarly called Four o'clock, because it opens only at tea time and shuts itself up again before breakfast. It is an old-fashioned herbaceous plant, seldom seen now, but quite decorative with its mixed colouring of yellow, white, red, or lilac, sometimes striped and flaked like some carnations. It can be grown as a half-hardy annual from seed sown in spring, and if you want to save the roots you will have to lift them in autumn like a dahlia. It seems simpler to grow it from seed afresh each year. Messrs. Thompson & Morgan sell the seed.

Then there is the Obedient Plant, *Physostegia virginiana*. The form of amusement provided by this object is the readiness of its flowers to remain in any position you choose to push them round the stem. I never could get it to work,

c

until a Scottish friend told me that I did not poosh it hard
enough. If you look carefully, you will see that they have
a sort of little hinge. A hardy perennial, of stiff habit, it
grows about two feet high and flowers at a useful time in
late summer. The variety usually offered by nurserymen
is called *Vivid*, but to my mind this is not a very pleasing
shade of pink. For those who share my distaste for pink
tinged with magenta, there is a white form, *alba*. Seed
from Thompson & Morgan, or plants from Messrs. Barr,
1s. 9d. each.

Perhaps the oddest plant of all is The Monarch of the
East, *Sauromatum guttatum*. The name comes from *saurus*,
a lizard, and *guttatum* means dotted or spotted. The flower,
which resembles an arum lily in shape, is indeed dotted
and spotted like some oriental lizards, only in different
colours. The Monarch rejoices in the decadent livery of
green and purple, with purple bruises on the pale green.
Its colouring, however, is not the chief queer thing about
it. The chief queer thing is the way it will agree to grow.
You set the tuber down on a saucer, just like that, plonk!
with no soil and no water, and quite soon it will begin
to sprout, and within a few weeks will begin to show signs
of flowering.

When it has flowered, you should plant the tuber out
in a rather damp corner of the garden to let it develop its
leaves during the summer. Then in August or September
you lift the tuber, dry it off, and eventually put it back
into its saucer, when it will perform again, year after year.
The first tuber will cost you half a crown, but you should
get many offsets if you want to increase your stock to give
birthday presents to your nephews and nieces, or even to
your own children, for the nursery window-sill. Mr. Ralph
Cusack, whose address will be found on p. 175, sells the
bulb; I have not seen it listed elsewhere.

February 1, 1953

Is anybody, or perhaps everybody, suffering as we are suffering from the inexplicable mischief of birds? One always expected to find the bullfinches busy among the fruit-blossom, but never until this year and last have I found the ground beneath the forsythias green as a lawn with pecked-off buds. There will not be a single smudge of yellow on them this spring. The winter-sweet was likewise stripped; and a neighbour tells me that every bud on her *Magnolia stellata* has been taken. It is not the bullfinches I complain of, but the sparrows. Can any ornithologist provide an explanation? The countrymen seem to think that the intensive spraying of orchards has destroyed so much of the birds' natural food in the shape of insects and grubs that they must turn elsewhere for nourishment. I love birds, but my affection is rapidly diminishing. I am told that spraying a plant with alum and water is a deterrent, but then one would have to repeat the dose after every shower of rain.

Meanwhile the snowdrops will soon be going over, and it is as well to remember that the time to divide them is immediately after they have finished flowering, and consequently to plant new bulbs also in March, if you can induce the bulb merchant to send them then. It is as well to remember, moreover, that there are different kinds besides the common snowdrop (only one hates to call it common). For instance, there is the finer variety called *Galanthus nivalis viridi-apice*, or green-tipped; and, of course, there is the double snowdrop, but I hope nobody would wish to grow that, for surely the whole beauty lies in the perfection of line of the single bell. Then there is the tall, large-flowered *Galanthus Elwesii*, from the hills behind Smyrna, often seen in old cottage gardens but not so often planted by the modern gardener, a most graceful dangling thing, flowering rather later than the little

Galanthus nivalis, the milk-flower of the snow. For people
who want something really unusual, and are prepared to
pay for it, there is *Galanthus Ikariae,* which has the
romantic peculiarity of growing in a wild state in only
one place in the world: the small island of Ikaria or Nikaria
in the Aegean sea, where Hercules buried the ill-fated
Icarus. It flowers in March, and much resembles the
common snowdrop, except that the flower is a little larger
and the leaves curl over backwards.

This by no means exhausts the list (there are fourteen
different species), but if anyone should have so perverted
a taste as to desire the sight of a snowdrop in autumn,
there is *Galanthus Olgae,* which comes from Mount
Taygetus, near Sparta, and flowers in October. The leaves
come after the flower; and this is a bulb which should
positively be planted during the spring months. I fancy
that it is the same as *Galanthus octobriensis,* under another
name.

Galanthus corcyrensis, from Corfu, flowers in November,
and *G. silicicus,* from Syria and Asia Minor, in December.

February 8, 1953
A letter from America reminds me that people who
wish to grow the ornamental gourds this summer should
order the seeds now. Sutton & Sons, Reading, stock them,
as also does Miss Hunter, see p. 177, and they can be had
in a variety of shapes and colours from the great orange
pumpkins (*potirons*), so familiar a sight as they lie hugely
about in the fields of France, to the little striped white-
and-green, no larger than a tennis ball. They should be
grown under the same conditions as the vegetable marrow;
picked when ripe; and lightly varnished with Copal varnish
to preserve them for indoor amusement throughout the
winter.

It appears that there is a Gourd Society in North

Carolina. Our American friends never do things by halves; and although their fondness for a tricksy ingenuity may sometimes outrun ours, I thought I might pass on some of their ideas for the benefit of those who have the leisure and the inclination to carry them out. Thus the elongated Dutchman's Pipe gourd may be scooped out and transformed into a ladle. The circular, medium-sized kinds may be scooped out likewise and turned into bowls. A pleasant occupation for an invalid, possibly—what an extract from an American catalogue calls "Fun for the shut-in."

* * *

The supreme example of North Carolinan ingenuity comes from one competitor in the Society's exhibition. She had turned a vast pumpkin into a coach for Cinderella, drawn by eight mouse-sized gourds. What a hint for our Women's Institutes, at their autumn Produce Show, in this Coronation year!

More pleasing to our taste, perhaps, is the harvest festival the Gourd Society organizes for the thousands of people who flock to see it. Throughout the summer, members of the Society have grown ornamental grasses to mix with their gourds; and this reminds me that I had always wanted to grow a patch of *Phalaris canariensis*, in plain English, Canary seed, in my garden, partly for fun, partly because I could then give a dollop of seed to any friend who kept a canary, and partly and principally because this form of Shakers or Quaking Grass, whose 'floures do continually tremble and shake, in such sort that it is not possible with the most steadfast hand to hold it from shaking,' was called in the first Elizabethan reign, when writers had some sense of vivid naming, the *Petty Panick*. We suffer from so many major panics nowadays that it is comforting to consider a petty one for a change.

February 15, 1953

Children have a gift for asking apparently simple questions to which there is no real answer. I was asked: 'What is your favourite flower?' The reply seemed almost to suggest itself: 'Any flower, turn by turn, which happens to be in season at the moment.'

Thus, I now find myself regretting that I did not plant more of the species crocuses which are busy coming out in quick succession. They are so very charming, and so very small. If you can go and see them in a nursery garden or at a flower show, do take the opportunity to make a choice. Grown in bowls or Alpine pans they are enchanting for the house; they recall those miniature works of art created by the great Russian artificer Fabergé in the luxurious days when the very rich could afford such extravagances. Grown in stone troughs out of doors, they look exquisitely in scale with their surroundings, since in open beds or even in pockets of a rockery they are apt to get lost in the vast areas of landscape beyond. One wants to see them close to the eye, fully to appreciate the pencilling on the outside of the petals; it seems to have been drawn with a fine brush, perhaps wielded by some sure-handed Chinese calligrapher, feathering them in bronze or in lilac. Not the least charm of these little crocuses is their habit of throwing up several blooms to a stem (it is claimed for *Ancyrensis* that a score will grow from a single bulb). Just when you think they are going off, a fresh crop appears.

Ancyrensis, from Ankara and Asia Minor, yellow, is usually the first to flower in January or early February, closely followed by *chrysanthus* and its seedlings *E. A. Bowles*, yellow and brown; *E. P. Bowles*, a deeper yellow feathered with purple; *Moonlight*, sulphur yellow and cream; *Snow Bunting*, cream and lilac; *Warley White*, feathered with purple. That fine species, *Imperati*, from Naples and Calabria, is slightly larger, violet-blue and straw-coloured; it flowers in February. *Susianus*, February and March, is well known as the Cloth of Gold crocus; *Sieberi*, a Greek, lilac-blue, is also well known; but *Suterianus* and its seedling *Jamie* are less often seen. Jamie must be the tiniest of all: a pale violet with deeper markings on the outside, he is no more than the size of a shilling across when fully expanded, and two inches high. I measured.

I have mentioned only a few of this delightful family, which should, by the way, be planted in August.*

February 23, 1953

The courage of some small and apparently fragile flowers never ceases to amaze me. Here are we humans, red-nosed and blue-cheeked in the frost and the snow, looking dreadfully plain; but there are the little flowers coming up, as brave and gay as can be, unaffected by snow or frost. The winter aconite is a cheerful resister, coming through the white ground with puffs of snow all over his bright burnished face, none the worse in his January–February beauty, and increasing from self-sown seedlings year after year.

We all grow the Algerian iris—and I wish, by the way, that I could find a nurseryman who lists it in separate varieties, for there is no doubt that some clumps flower much earlier than others, even in November, whereas others do not arrive until March, and also there is a considerable difference in the colour, ranging from the usual pale lavender to a really fine deep purple. (According to William Robinson, this richly coloured variety would appear to be *speciosa*.) I imagine that the explanation lies in their place of origin, for Algeria is not their only native home, and they are to be found also in Greece, in Asia Minor, in Syria, and even so far east as the coast of the

* Messrs. Wallace specialize in them. See p. 175 for the address.

Black Sea. It is, however, not of this iris that I wished to
write, but of the less familiar *Iris histrioides*, which to my
mind has many advantages over *I. unguicularis*, or, as most
people call it, *stylosa*. It is true that *histrioides* does not
give us a prolonged flowering period, but flowers only once,
in February, so that we cannot look forward to picking
for many weeks in succession. Once we have granted
stylosa the superiority in this respect, there is nothing but
good to say of the brilliantly blue little actor from the north
of Asia Minor. For one thing, it blooms before the leaves
have come through, and even when the leaves do appear
they are far neater than the frankly unsightly muddle
which makes us relegate *stylosa* to a hidden corner. For
another thing, the cobalt of its petals is intense and its
capacity for resistance to the weather is unequalled. For
three weeks now my small group has been exposed without
any protection to gales and rain and cold and snow; I have
daily expected to find it sodden or tattered, but the valiant
little thing—it is only four inches high, though the flower
is comparatively large, much larger than its relation
I. reticulata—has never faltered.

If it is happy, in a sunny place with some mortar rubble
to provide it with lime, it should increase by means of the
offsets which will form round the parent bulb; and as
Iris histrioides is not at all easy to buy now, even at 5s.
a bulb it is advisable to preserve the offsets and grow them
on in pots until they attain their flowering size, which
may be in a year or two. This sort of gardening demands
time and love, I know; but how great is the satisfaction
and the reward.

March

March 4, 1951

A WINTER corner. . . . Winter must here be taken as meaning January to the end of March. I wish we had a name for that intermediate season which includes St. Valentine's Day, February 14th, and All Fools' Day, April 1st. It is neither one thing nor the other, neither winter nor spring. Could we call it wint-pring, which has a good Anglo-Saxon sound about it, and accept it, like marriage, for better or worse?

My wint-pring corner shall be stuffed with every sort of bulb or corm that will flower during those few scanty weeks. The main point is that it shall be really stuffed; crammed full; packed tight. The winter aconite (January–February) will flower first, with *Narcissus minimus*, sometimes called *Asturiensis*, coming up amongst it, and also the sky blue *Muscari azureus*. There will be the spring flowering crocuses; there will be *Iris reticulata*, the ordinary purple and gold sort, and the earlier flowering blue kind called *Cantab*; and the black-green *Iris tuberosa*; and I might also risk half a dozen *Iris histrioides*, not very reliable but so lovely that it is worth taking a chance.

There will be many miniature daffodils, and if anyone is particularly interested in these I would advise him to go to the R.H.S. spring shows, where a Cornish bulb-grower, Mr. Alec Gray, of Treswithian Daffodil Farm, Camborne, always devotes his stall to these tiny, exquisite things. There will be some early tulips, such as *Tulipa biflora* and

turkestanica and *Kaufmaniana*, the water-lily tulip, flowering in March. There will be *Scilla biflora* and *Scilla Tubergeniana*, both flowering in February; and as a ground work,
to follow after the winter aconites, I shall cram the ground
with the Greek *Anemone blanda*, opening her starry blue
flower in the rare sun of February, and with the Italian
Anemone Apennina, who comes a fortnight later and carries
on into March and is at her best in April. Terrible spreaders,
these anemones; but so blue a carpet may gladly be allowed
to spread.

If only *Cyclamen coum* were not so expensive, at 5s. a
corm, I would like to include him, but at that price he
is only for the millionaires. (The alternative is to grow
him from seed; slower, but quite satisfactory in the end.)
Otherwise, the winter corner should be cheap to plant;
and needs, humbly, only a little patch of ground where
you can find one. Let it be in a place which you pass
frequently, and can observe from day to day.

March 11, 1951

A friend of mine, whose own fingers are of the greenest,
reproaches me from time to time for making gardening
sound too easy. My optimism, she says, is misleading. Yet
I try to avoid recommending 'difficult' plants, or at any
rate to accompany them always with a warning. The truth
is probably that most plants are temperamental, except the
weeds, which all appear to be possessed of magnificent
constitutions. The mystery of the Madonna lily, for
instance, has never been satisfactorily explained. *Daphne
mezereum* provides another puzzle: you may observe all the
rules, but nothing will make her flourish if she does not
intend to do so. Then there is the case of the self-sown
seedling, which, sprouting up in apparently impossible
conditions, excels in health and vigour anything similar

which you may have transplanted with the greatest care into a prepared bed of the most succulent consistency.

In my own garden I have a curious example of the perverse behaviour of plants. Two cuttings of a poplar, brought home in a sponge-bag from Morocco, were both struck and planted out at the same time. Same age, same parent, same aspect, same soil; yet, fifteen years later, one is only half the size of the other. Why? I can suppose only that like two children of identical begetting and upbringing, they differ in constitution and character.

It thus becomes evident that gardening, unlike mathematics, is not an exact science. It would be dull if it were. Naturally, there are certain laws whose transgression means disaster: you would not plant an azalea in a chalk pit. I do agree with my friend, however, that writers on gardening very often omit to make some elementary comments, pointing out possible causes of failure. This brings me to two things I wanted to say. The first is about snowdrops. The time to move them, if you wish to do so, is just after they have flowered; in other words, now. (Do not cut off their heads as they are very generous in seeding themselves.) The second thing is about mice. They eat bulbs, leaving large bare patches where one has planted snowdrops and crocuses. I asked an eminent nurseryman what one could do about this, and he replied that as one soaked peas in red lead before sowing them, he could see no reason why the same procedure should harm bulbs. It would be an experiment worth trying, because there is no doubt that distressing gaps do appear, for which I can find no explanation except mice. Besides, there are tell-tale little holes.

I am ashamed of having forgotten to mention the blue anemone hepatica as occupants of a winter corner, last week. They should on no account be omitted.

March 18, 1951

The Dog's-tooth violets (*Erythronium dens-canis*) should now be coming into flower, so this is the time to study these curly objects and to decide if you would like to order some for planting next autumn. There will probably be a fine display of them at the Royal Horticultural Society's fortnightly spring shows when anybody living within reach of Vincent Square, Westminster, can go and spend an hour of pure delight at this débutante festival. Of course one must expect everything to look better at a show than it will ever look in one's own garden. The exhibitors have chosen their best specimens, and have arranged them in a very becoming bed of moist dark-brown-velvet peat, showing them up to their best advantage.

The Dog's-tooth violets should be there, beneath the great flowering cherries and almonds of the spring. They are small, they are low, they are humble in stature, not more than six inches high, but with their beautifully mottled leaves and reflexed petals like tiny martagon lilies they are more than worthy of their place. Some of them are natives of central Europe, some of North America; they belong to the lily family and have nothing to do with violets. 'Dog's-tooth' is because of the tuber, which is white and pointed, like a fang. They prefer a little shade; light woodland is ideal for them; they like some sand and peat or leaf mould in their soil, which should be moist but never waterlogged; they dislike being moved, so leave them alone for years once they have settled down. I have seen them flourishing and increasing even under beech-trees, where few things will grow. You can get them in white, pink, purple, and yellow. They are inexpensive, at about 4s. a dozen (see illustration opposite p. 64).

The trilliums, or North American wood-lily, also called the Trinity Flower from its triangular shape, flower a little later but enjoy the same conditions of shade and soil. One does not very often see them, but I notice that they always attract attention. Claret-coloured or white, they grow to about a foot high and have the advantage of lasting a very long time, which seems to be true of most woodland things, I suppose because they do not get burnt up by a hot sun. Unfortunately the trilliums are rather expensive, at 3s. 6d. each according to my catalogues; but as they are very striking, a group of only three or four makes quite an effect, and after all one can always add a couple every year. They, as well as the Dog's-tooth violets, are ideal not only for woodland planting but also for a cool shaded place in a rock garden.

The claret-coloured one is *Trillium erectum.* The white one is *Trillium grandiflorum*, which in its native home is known as Wake Robin, a name we commonly give to our wild arum or Lords-and-Ladies.

March 25, 1951

Easter-day, loveliest and youngest of feasts. I can hardly bring myself to think about summer, which to me always seems middle-aged compared with the adolescence of March, April, and even May. March is seventeen, though by no means always sweet; April is eighteen; May is nineteen; June is twenty to twenty-five; and then July leaps to thirty and thirty-five; and then August from forty to fifty; September to a mature, mellow sixty; October to an even mellower, yellower seventy; and then comes the leafless calm of the descending year.

Still, one must be practical, thinking of summer, if one is to fill up the gaps in one's garden, and I have been forcing myself to think about it in terms of the *hemerocallis*, or day-lily. This used to be regarded as a common old plant, almost a weed, when we grew the type which spread everywhere and was only a pale orange thing, not worth having. Now there are many fine hybrids, which may come as a revelation to those who have not yet seen them. They may be ordered now, for planting within the next two or three weeks, so this is the time to obtain them.

Some of them are to be had at very high prices, right up to £2 each for named varieties, but you need not pay that price for a collection of the hybrids. You can get them at 27s. 6d. a dozen for mixed hybrids. The firm of Amos Perry, of Enfield, Middlesex, has been responsible for much good hybridizing; and further fine varieties have been raised in America. They will grow either in sun or shade. They will grow in damp soil, even by the waterside if you are so fortunate as to have a stream or a pond in your garden, when their trumpets of amber, apricot, orange, ruddle, and Venetian red will double themselves in reflection in the water. They will grow equally well in an ordinary bed or border. They are, in fact, extremely obliging plants, thriving almost anywhere.

They are especially useful for the summer garden, flowering as they do from July into September. Mostly in July and August.

My search for an alphabetical glossary of botanical terms has been rewarded by the discovery of exactly what I wanted. *A Popular Dictionary of Botanical Names and Terms, with their English Equivalents*, by George F. Zimmer, is published by Routledge and Kegan Paul, Ltd., Broadway House, 68–74, Carter Lane, E.C.4, at the very reasonable cost of 5s.

March 2, 1952

It sometimes happens that people inherit, or acquire, an old dwelling house or cottage with a pool or even with the remains of a moat. Presumably, such surroundings are highly picturesque, and the fortunate owner wants to make the most of them. Let us assume also that no previous

owner has bothered about suitable planting, and has left
the waterside to ramp away into a terrible mess of unworthy
weeds. So I thought I would devote my next two articles
to this rather special problem.

Water is the making of a garden. It gives a rare chance
to the gardener. He can grow things *in* the water, and
beside the water, and even *on* the water—a triple pleasure,
far more agreeable than the filling up of triplicate forms.
I will take *in* and *on* the water first, and leave the higher
marginal planting until next week.

Water-lilies come first to the mind; and apart from the
white and our native yellow one, there are hybrids in pink,
red, and primrose. Twelve to eighteen inches of water-
depth is a safe rough guide, and full sun. The usual method
is to sink the plants in an old basket, when they will root
through the basket into the bottom mud; but they can
also be tied between two turves and sunk (the right way
up). Late May or early June is the time. If you think the
leaves of waterlilies too large for a small pond, there is,
the Water Hawthorn, *Aponogeton*, also the Bog-bean
with small white flowers, floating; or *Villarsia*, with
golden flowers four inches above the water level, or
Pontederia cordata, like a pale blue arum. For the edges,
where the water is not so deep, our native yellow flag iris
is both lovely and reliable; the Flowering Rush, *Butomus
umbellatus*, is an arrowy grower three to four feet high
with rosy flowers; it looks exotic, but is in fact to be found
wild in Britain. *Sagittaria*, the true Arrow-head, white
flowers, associates well with this rather spiky group.

For something lower in stature on the boggy margin,
the water Forget-me-not, *Myosotis palustris*, is a great
spreader of a china-blue, paler than the garden varieties.
The King Cup or Marsh Marigold will grow either in sun
or shade, which is obliging of it.

Finally, the very brave could experiment with the

ordinary white arum, the Lily of the Nile, which, if planted deep enough, should survive an average winter in the South of England. But if you want to grow arums out of doors in water, the Bog-arum, *Calla palustris*, is a less risky investment.

March 9, 1952

In choosing plants for the waterside, I think it is important to remember that their beauty will be doubled if you can arrange for them to be reflected in the water. If the water is covered by floating plants, such as water-lilies, this will not be possible, though one can usually contrive to keep a bare zone round the outside to serve as a mirror. Much will depend, of course, on whether the pond has banked-up sides, or fades away into a swampy level; these are differences which can only be considered on the spot.

For the marshy swamp I would suggest a drift of the moisture-loving primulas: *Sikkimensis, Florindae, Japonica, Chionantha, Bulleyana, Helodoxa*, known as the Glory of the Marsh. If economy is a consideration, as it usually is, these primulas are all easily raised from seed. The tall clematis-like Japanese irises, *I. Kaempferi*, look most beautiful growing amongst them, but I always think their requirements are a little awkward to manage—wet in summer, dry in winter. Nature's water supply usually works the other way round. The blue *Iris laevigata*, on the other hand, does not mind boggy conditions all the year through. *Iris Sibirica*, less large and handsome than the Japanese, is exceedingly graceful and pretty and most accommodating, though it does not like being too deeply drowned. *Iris Delvayi* resembles it, and is useful because it flowers later, when *Sibirica* is over. The richer the soil, the better for all these irises, even to a mulch of rotted manure.

These are all tall-growing, but if you can spare a special corner, marking it off with a ring of rough stones, do try the little almost-black gold-veined *I. chrysographes*, a real gem; and *I. fulva*, a coppery-red.

So much for the waterside irises, but coming higher up on the bank, assuming that there is a bank, and that it is dry, I think one might plant the scarlet dog wood *Cornus alba*. Do not be misled by the name; *alba* in this case refers only to the flowers, which are silly, contemptible little things in summer. The glory of this plant is the red bark of its bare stems throughout the winter. Caught by the light of the sinking sun, reflected in water, it is as warming to the heart as a log-fire on the hearth after a cold day.

March 16, 1952

The other evening I had a strange and lovely experience. I found myself, never mind how or why, completely alone in the Royal Horticultural Society's hall in Vincent Square after the fortnightly show had been closed to the public for the night. There I was, by myself, with not so much as a stray kitten wandering about. The lights were on, turning that vast hall into a raftered church overhead, and shining down on the silent flowers beneath. It was like being in a cathedral paved with flowers, with the scent of thousands of hyacinths taking the place of incense. An old phrase from the fifteenth century came into my mind: 'The fair flourished fields of flowers and of herbs, whereof the breath as of balm blows in our nose, that ilk sensitive soul must surely delight.'

I write this, however, not so much to describe that experience as to urge you to take note now of the many small bulbous plants which grace this time of the year. The tiny crocus species, for instance, some so delicately feathered on their outer petals with a complementary colour—*C. susianus*, yellow feathered with brown, or

D

C. chrysanthus Snow Bunting, white feathered with lavender. They are too numerous for separate mention here,
but a good catalogue will give a descriptive list if you
cannot manage to visit a nursery or a flower show. Messrs.
R. Wallace, Tunbridge Wells, have a very long list. (See
also under February 15, 1952.) Cheap to buy, they should,
I think, be crowded all together into a special corner, or
grown in a stone sink, or for the house in an Alpine pan.
The miniature narcissi go well with them, and, of course,
the small irises; there is a particularly fine wine-red form
of *I. reticulata* called J. S. Dijt. The early grape hyacinth,
Muscari azureus, mixes its sky-blue spikes to perfection,
it is nearly the same colour as *I. reticulata Cantab*.

The rest of this brilliant little company should not be
too ruinous. A few shillings will go a long way for a start,
and one can always add more during ensuing years. They
take up so little room, and are so welcome in the months
when spring seems to be so endlessly laggard.

March 22, 1952

Many years ago, in the high mountains of Persia, I
collected some seed pods off a mimosa which was most
unaccountably growing there, some 5,000 feet above sea-
level, and some hundred miles from any spot whence it
could possibly be considered as a garden escape. I do not
pretend to explain how it came there, in that cold, stony,
snowy, desolate region; all I know is that there it was, and
that I brought seeds home, and now have a tree of it
growing out of doors in my garden and a vase full of it
on my table, smelling not of the snows but of the warm
south.

I think it is probably *Acacia dealbata* and not a true
mimosa at all, but it looks so like what we call mimosa in
the florists' shops or on the French Riviera that the name
may conveniently serve. Botanists may write to tell me

that it is more likely to be *Albizzia Julibrissin*, a native of Persia, whereas the acacia is a native of Australia, which adds to the mystery of how it came to be growing on the Elburz mountains; but *Albizzia* it certainly is not.

All this preamble is intended to suggest that enterprising gardeners in the South of England might well risk a plant in a sheltered corner. Of course the ideal place is a large conservatory, but few people have large conservatories nowadays. It might not come unscathed through a terrible winter such as we had in 1947, but my tree at any rate has not so far turned a hair in frost, and the place where I found it growing was certainly more bleak and windswept than anything we can provide here. We take the precaution of wrapping its trunk and lower branches in trousers of sacking, and that is all the protection it gets. For greater safety, it could be trained fan-wise against a wall, if you started the training young enough. I should perhaps add that a high wall selters it from the north, and that it is planted facing full south. I should add also that it is no good picking it before the flowers are fully out, in the hope that they will open in water; there are some things which refuse to oblige in that way, and this is one of them. You must wait till the clusters are as fluffy and yellow as ducklings.

It makes a charming pot plant until it becomes too large and has to be transferred into a tub or else planted out into the open ground.

Anyone wanting to try the experiment can get this acacia from Treseder's Nurseries, Truro.

March 30, 1952

Nostalgia for the past has brought with it a revival of taste for the old-fashioned flowers: the flaked pinks and carnations, the double primroses, the old roses, the broken tulips, the double Sweet William. Perhaps it is not only nostalgia for an age which, rightly or wrongly, we esteem to have been happier than our own, as it was certainly more leisurely, but also a natural reaction against the exaggerated blooms we are offered to-day: size not subtlety. Who wants a begonia like a saucer?

Amongst the many plants thus returning to favour, the auricula finds its little place. I am not here concerned with the outdoor, or Alpine, auricula, so familiar in cottage gardens, but with what is known as the *Show auricula*, which must be grown indoors or under glass, not because it fails in hardiness but because the powder (*farina*) gets washed off in the rain and all its essentially cleanly character is lost. It cannot afford to get itself into a mess. Neatest and most exquisitely demarcated of flowers, it must keep itself as trim as the fireside cat. Given this opportunity, it will produce in April and May flowerheads which combine at one and the same time a demure simplicity and an appearance of extreme sophistication. Grey; green; white edged with green; scarlet edged with green; yellow edged with grey; the variations are manifold. The old growers used to put their pots on ranged shelves, sometimes fitted into a small home-made theatre with scenery painted behind it as a background.

Few of us have the leisure to indulge in such charming fancies, but it is still possible to treat ourselves to a hanging wall-brackets with four or five shelves, knocked up from some odd pieces of wood by any handy carpenter.

To be practical about raising the auriculas. They are expensive to buy as plants, but cheap to grow from a packet of seed from the best firm. Sow in April in a pan of very finely sifted soil, and scarcely cover the seed. This is important: if too deeply buried the seed will refuse to germinate. Prick the seedlings out into tiny pots, and pot up singly into four-inch pots, never into a big pot. Keep them cool always, never exposed to a hot sun.

The House of Douglas, Edenside, Great Bookham, Surrey, supply seed.

March 8, 1953

I have just planted out a *Metasequoia glyptostroboides*. In case this name should by any chance sound unfamiliar, I should explain that it refers to a tree whose discovery was one of the romances of plant-collecting. It had been known for some time as a fossil going back to the Mesozoic era which I understand occurred some two hundred million years ago, but as no living specimen had ever been seen, botanists assumed that it had gone out of existence at about the same time as its contemporaries the giant reptiles. The surprise of a Mr. T. Wang can therefore be imagined, when in the year 1946 three strange conifers were observed growing in a remote valley of north-eastern Szechuan. Their foliage corresponded to his fossil remains. Further exploration revealed the somewhat patchy presence of more, similar trees in the same area, growing for the most part beside streams in marshy places; seed was collected, and, since it germinates readily, this extraordinary survivor from a fantastically distant age may now be regarded as safe for future generations in Europe and America.

It seems unlikely that many owners of small gardens will feel inspired to plant one, for its eventual height of 130 feet may prove as intimidating as its name. Nevertheless, as young specimens can already be seen growing in some public and some private gardens, I might as well describe their appearance so that you can recognize a *Metasequoia* when you meet one. Pale green and feathery in spring and summer, it turns bright pink in autumn, a really startling sight when the sunshine catches it. Judging by my own experience from a tiny seedling given to me, it grows very fast, about six feet in as many years, especially if planted in the damp situation it loves.

I did not plant mine in a damp situation; I kept it in a pot, not knowing what to do with it; and it grew and grew, becoming more and more pot-bound, poor thing, but still thriving. It throve so well under these unkind conditions that I felt bound to reward it by letting it out into a damp gully in the middle of a field, where, if no cow eats it, I shall watch its progress with considerable interest.

If any brave person, or any enterprising municipal council, wants one of these living fossils, it can be obtained at a price varying from 15s. 6d. to £3 3s. 0d., according to size. Messrs. Hillier supply them.

April

April 1, 1951

THIS, I fear, is not going to be a very practical article. It will be of no use at all to anybody who is making or planting a garden. But as it will appear on All Fools' Day I may perhaps be allowed a frivolity for once.

The frivolity concerns a nurseryman's catalogue dated 1838. Queen Victoria had recently come to the throne. One of her humbler subjects, Mr. John Miller, of the Durdham Down Nursery, near Bristol, had just died as a bankrupt. His executors were carrying on his Business, for the benefit of the Creditors including the Bankrupt's immediate Relatives.

Poor Mr. John Miller. He had a magnificent list of plants for disposal, not only roses, but pelargoniums, auriculas, pinks, orchids, herbaceous plants—pages and pages of them. It seems a shame that he should go smash so soon after his young Queen had embarked on a reign of over sixty years of prosperity. He should have prospered with her; evidently he did not.

The reason why I here revive his list is not so much because I feel sorry for Mr. Miller, dead and lost 113 years ago, as because I think his catalogue may interest rose specialists and may also appeal to those who share my appreciation for such names as these, picked at random:—

Monstrous four seasons; Belle sans flatterie; Black African; La belle Junon; Ninon de l'Enclos; Temple d'Apollon; Conque de Venus.

Where have they gone, these bearers of fantastically romantic names? If Edmond Rostand had known of them he would surely have put a great speech about them into the mouth of Cyrano de Bergerac. Where are they now? Lost, I suppose, for ever, unless they could be discovered in some ancient garden in England or France.

One of those queer quirks of memory that sometimes assail us made me take down from my shelves a copy of *The Rose Fancier's Manual*, translated from the French by Mrs. Gore, once a best-seller amongst novelists. I found, as I expected, that Mrs. Gore's book exactly corresponded in date, 1838, with the list of Mr. Miller, deceased. She mentions a number of the same roses, but she also mentions others which Mr. Miller had not got, or perhaps had sold out of. Her *Coupe d'amour* does not figure in Mr. Miller's list; nor does *Tout aimable*; nor does the rose whose name, if truthful, makes me want to possess it more than any: *Rien ne me surpasse*.

Surely the most exacting should be satisfied with that.

April 8, 1951

Vegetables. . . . Not cabbages or turnips or parsnips, sodden in water, insipid, tasteless, 'one mutt, two veg.,' but rare, succulent vegetables which are quite as easy to grow. Most of them can be sown this month or next, and can be obtained from Miss Kathleen Hunter, who is the successor of the well-known Miss Eleanour Sinclair Rohde. Address on p. 177.

Calabrese is perhaps becoming better known, but is still not well known enough. It is a brassica much appreciated in America and with good reason. It serves a double purpose, because you first eat the small, cauliflower-like head, which is green instead of white, and then you keep continuously picking the side-shoots, which taste of asparagus. It is really and truly delicious, and most prolific. Sow seed in the open in April, or buy plants at 10s. a hundred, 25 for 3s., to be delivered June–July. It likes a rich soil, with manure.

Peas. Have you tried the *True French petit pois*, or the *Mange-tout*, which is so tender that you eat the whole thing, pod and all? 1s. a packet each.

Beans. The Golden butter-bean, a dwarf which needs no stringing. Sow it towards the end of May, and pick it when it is lemon yellow. 6d. a packet.

Onions. Have you the Tree-onion? It is a perennial, and grows its little edible onions at the top of the plant instead of in the ground. Plants cost 1s. each, or 11s. a dozen, and can be increased by planting out the little onions or by division of the roots.

Lettuce. Two of the best lettuces, I think, are *Brittle Ice* and *Green Jade*, nice names and crisp hearts. *Green Jade* may seem rather expensive at 2s. 6d. a packet, but it is exceptionally good. It should be sown at frequent intervals, because it is inclined to bolt, and it should never be transplanted, only thinned out. *Brittle Ice* costs less, at 6d. a packet. Both are of the cabbage type, not the Cos. Why anybody bothers to grow the Cos instead of the solid, curly cabbage sorts passes my understanding.

These are all more or less necessary vegetables, meaning that one must have brassicas, peas, beans, onions, and lettuce, in one variety or another, but there are many other things which the enterprising kitchen-gardener might grow as extras. *Hamburg Parsley*, for instance, of which you eat the root, grated or sliced, in salads, when it tastes like nuts; it will keep all through the winter. Sow in April, seed at 1s. a packet. The *Black Radish* can also be stored throughout the winter, 'big as a tennis ball, with a skin as black as soot and flesh as white as snow.' Sow in July, 1s. 6d. a packet.

Squashes and marrows ought to come into this article, but space runs out. I shall return to them next week, with a note on the ornamental gourds. Meanwhile I must ask forgiveness from many correspondents who urged me to write an article about window-boxes or hanging baskets in town. I tried, but it was such a poor article that I tore it up. I don't know anything about town gardening; I have never had any experience of it; I am a country gardener not a town gardener; and if one values one's integrity in such matters one cannot pretend to a knowledge one does not possess. Sorry; but there it is.

April 15, 1951

Ornamental or edible, the great family of the *Cucurbitaceae* must have representatives in every garden. We all grow *Cucurbita Pepo ovifera*. Do we? Yes, but we don't call it by that name: we call it the vegetable marrow. And how wrongly we treat it! Instead of picking and cooking it when it is only about four inches long, we encourage it to grow into something resembling a porpoise, a prize-winner at the local flower-show but a soapy, watery thing in the kitchen.

In this article I want to suggest some other types of the family. Have you, for example, ever tried growing the *Avocadella?*—not to be confused with the Avocado peas. You grow it as you would grow a marrow, but its fruit never grows bigger than a grapefruit in size. It will cost you 2s. 6d. a packet of seed. Sow it now, under glass, if you have glass; if not, sow it out of doors at the end of May. It likes a sunny place, and some manure in the soil. An old compost heap suits it nicely.

Then there is the *Apple cucumber*. This is a novelty I really recommend. Most prolific, it produces egg-sized fruits more constantly and reliably than any hen. Sow it in a frame now, or in the open in May. Seed costs 1s. 6d. a packet.

Then there are the *Cocozelle*. These are the *Zucchini* of Italy, well known to all travellers in that delectable country.

You can get the seed at 1s. a packet, and grow it as you would grow a marrow. Then if you like squashes, you can now get the *Hubbard Squash* at 1s. a packet, or the *Custard Marrow* at 6d. a packet.

This is all very practical, culinary, and utilitarian. I would now like to put in a word for the ornamental gourds, which are no good to eat but which are just sheer fun. And what fun they are! What jokes! What fantasies! You get a mixture in a seed packet and you may get all shapes, colours, and sizes. Little turbans, little striped green-and-yellows, or round oranges; you may get, if you are lucky, named sorts, such as the *Warted Gourd*, the *Bishop's Mitre*, the *Hedgehog*, the *Powder Flask*, the *Hercules Club*, or the *Turk's Cap*, white or red. Whatever comes out of your shilling packet you may be sure of variety; and you can preserve them throughout the winter for house-decoration in bowls if you varnish them with a thin coating of Copal varnish.

But, before doing that, grow them over any rough fence or shed this summer. They provide a very quick covering, which your neighbour is unlikely to have thought of. Miss Hunter, whose address will be found on p. 177, supplies seed of everything mentioned here.

April 22, 1951

However popular, however ubiquitous, the clematis must remain among the best hardy climbers in our gardens. Consider first their beauty, which may be either flamboyant or delicate. Consider their long flowering period, from April till November. Consider also that they are easy to grow; do not object to lime in the soil; are readily propagated, especially by layering; are very attractive even when not in flower, with their silky-silvery seedheads, which always remind me of Yorkshire terriers curled into a ball; offer an immense variety both of species and hybrids; and may be used in many different ways, for growing over sheds, fences, pergolas, hedges, old trees, or up the walls of houses. The perfect climber? Almost, but there are two snags which worry most people.

There is the problem of pruning. This, I admit, is complicated if you want to go into details, but as a rough working rule it is safe to say that those kinds which flower in the spring and early summer need pruning just after they have flowered, whereas the later flowering kinds (i.e., those that flower on the shoots they have made during the current season) should be pruned in the early spring. For further information I would refer you to Ernest Markham's book *Clematis*, which has just been republished by Country Life, Ltd., at 18s. and which includes a chapter on pruning by Mr. George Jackman, whose father raised the well-known *C. Jackmanii* and its many hybrids, or indeed to Mr. Jackman's own catalogue, obtainable from his nursery at Woking.

The second worry is *wilt*. You may prefer to call it *Ascochyta Clematidina*, but the result is the same, that your most promising plant will suddenly, without the slightest warning, be discovered hanging like miserable wet string. The cause is known to be a fungus, but the cure, which would be more useful to know, is unknown. The only comfort is that the plant will probably shoot up again from the root; you should, of course, cut the collapsed strands down to the ground to prevent any spread of the disease. It is important, also, to obtain plants on their own roots, for they are far less liable to attack. I see that Mr. Markham agrees with this.

Slugs, caterpillars, mice, and rabbits are all fond of young clematis, but that is just one of the normal troubles of gardening. Wilt is the real speciality of the clematis.

There is much more to be said about this beautiful plant but space only to say that it likes shade at its roots, and don't let it get too dry.

April 29, 1951

In these ruinous days many people would like to make a little profit back from their gardens. In fact so many people are now selling surplus flowers and vegetables that we shall soon be all sellers with no one left to buy. However, the market still exists, not only for the commercial grower but also for the amateur, and many a dark industrial city welcomes the golden bunch as a reminder that the daffodil blows somewhere in the orchards of the south.

It is to 'the man with a small income and a small garden' that a new little book, *Amateur Gardening for Pleasure and Profit*, by C. C. Vyvyan (Museum Press, 6s.), is addressed. The writer supposes a garden owner, anxious to obtain some information about the most saleable crop of flowers, fruits, or vegetables; how to pick and pack them; what kind of string and boxes to use; what policy to pursue (honesty is recommended), and, most important, how to find a market. As a start Lady Vyvyan favours local shops, hotels, friends and neighbours. This saves much cost in transport and packing materials, more especially if you can induce the customer to come and collect the produce from your own door; it also cuts out the commission exacted by the middleman. Direct selling, then, is the thing, until you become so ambitious that you start despatching weekly consignments to Covent Garden. I suspect also that Lady Vyvyan, although she does not explicitly say so, favours making use of friends and visitors who come in motor-cars. 'Oh, must you go? *Would* you mind dropping this bundle of holly for me? It isn't very prickly and it won't take you more than a mile out of your way.' Thus is a local business built up.

It is a really practical little book, written by someone with personal experience who knows the snags as well as the ropes. She is full of good hints. Did you realize, for instance, the marketable value of such 'common property' as ivy, ferns, or that weed the Winter Heliotrope, an invasive danger in the garden but a scented delight in January to those unfortunates who are condemned to live in towns? Or moss? Though, as Lady Vyvyan sagely says, moss-gathering is suitable only for a man with much leisure or for children and visitors who need to be given some harmless occupation. It takes too long for busy people. Rightly, she did not mention the rolling stone.

April 6, 1952

To the true plant lover, there are few treasures greater than those he has collected for himself, preferably on a holiday abroad. I know myself how preciously I value those few precarious survivors I have managed to bring home in the form of cuttings damply wrapped in my sponge-bag, or in the form of bulbs stuffed into the toe-caps of a pair of shoes. The foreign soil I found lingering, when next I put the shoes on, was not the least part of my pleasure. It might be gritty, but it was a bit of Persia, France, Italy, or Spain. These survivors are dearer to me than anything I could have ordered for paid shillings from a nurseryman. So, as Easter approaches and some people may be preparing to spend their £25 across the Channel, let me utter a word of warning.

I recently received a series of ecstatic letters from a traveller in Greece. 'I wish you could see,' he wrote, 'the hillsides here covered with anemones, narcissus, iris, jonquil, cyclamen. . . . I am digging a lot up, with the trowel I had the foresight to bring with me. Would you please ascertain from the Ministry of Agriculture what permit is necessary to import bulbs and corms into England? It would break my heart if, on arrival, I had to throw them all with a splash into the harbour at Dover.'

The Ministry of Agriculture was most courteously co-operative, granting the permit by return of post, on the understanding that the said bulbs or corms were for personal not commercial use; in other words, that the digger-up intended them only for his own garden. At the same time, it pointed out that a permit should, strictly speaking, have been obtained *before* the traveller left England. (Prospective plant-collectors, please note this important condition.)

The sad part of the story comes now. My traveller in Greece, who is no smuggler, had rightly foreseen the difficulty of getting his little parcels legitimately through the English Customs. What he had not foreseen was that they might be taken away from him by the Italian *Dogana* when he landed at Brindisi on his way home from Greece. Dozens of Greek bulbs therefore splashed, not into Dover harbour, but into the Adriatic Sea.

The moral of this article is: if you are going abroad, and want to bring plants home with you, make sure before you go what regulations apply in every country, not only in your own.

April 13, 1952

At this time of year, or even a month earlier, a few pans of small, brightly coloured flowers give vast pleasure. If you want to see what I mean, done on the grand scale, go to the Alpine House at Kew. No need to be so ambitious, for even half a dozen pans on the staging of a small greenhouse produce an effect of clean brilliance, which I suppose is enhanced by the light coming on all sides, and overhead, through glass; and also because each bloom is unsmirched by rain or soil-splash, unnibbled by slugs, and unpecked by birds. Furthermore, the greyness of the stone chippings with which you will, I hope, have sprinkled your pans, throws up the colours into strong relief. Ideally, the pans should be whitewashed, for no one can pretend that the red of a flowerpot is pleasing, or of an agreeable texture.

Some of the little primulas lend themselves very happily to this treatment, *P. marginata*, for instance, or the lovely pale lavender *Linda Pope*; or even a clump of the ordinary blue primrose which suffers so from the mischief of birds when growing out of doors in the garden. I would like also to see a pan of larger size, interplanted with some of the choicer varieties of common bulbs, coming up between the primulas: the intensely blue hanging bells of *Scilla Spring Beauty*, or the strange greenish-turquoise of the grape-hyacinth called *Tubergeniana* or the pale blue of *Chionodoxa gigantea*, which in spite of its adjectival name resembles a tiny lily. Endless variations could be played on different colour-schemes; you could have a cool pan of yellow prim-roses interplanted with the white grape-hyacinth and the white chionodoxa; or, for something looking rich and ecclesiastical, a pan of that very ordinary magenta *Primula Wanda* with the inky blue *Muscari latifolium* amongst it. The grey cushions of saxifrage, with their miniature pink or rosy flowers, look charming in low pans with some stones to set them off, but these, I think, should be grown by themselves, not interplanted.

It is too late this year, of course, and is an idea to materialize twelve months hence. It may be a bit of a time-taker for busy people, but a welcome occupation for an invalid or a convalescent. Meanwhile, do visit the Alpine House at Kew.

April 20, 1952

Several times in this column I have written about growing grapes out of doors. There are several hardy kinds which will do perfectly well, and ripen, either in the open or allowed to ramble over a porch or trained against a wall. Now comes Mr. Edward Hyams with a further suggestion: why not grow some under cloches? Many people

Pearson's Alexander.

Pomona Superba.   Count de Sellis.   Desdemona

use the big barn-type of cloche for tomatoes; why not spare a few for a row of vines?

All particulars about how this can be done will be found in his new book, *Grapes Under Cloches*, published by Faber and Faber, 12s. 6d., illustrated, with lists of suitable varieties and addresses where to obtain them. This interesting monograph also tells how to cope with diseases, how to make wine, how to turn grapes into raisins, and how to destroy wasps by a new method. Even if you do not wish to divert any cloches in order to become a vinearoon, which is Mr. Hyams's adopted translation of *vigneron*, you may still find a great deal of fascinating and sometimes amusing information. Did you, for instance, know that in Greek vineyards the two most redoubtable enemies are, not wasps or blackbirds, but tortoises and porcupines?

But the idea I really wanted to pick out of Mr. Hyams's book is the ancient idea of making a hedge of vines. To do this, you allow your young vine to develop only one single rod, which you train horizontally, along a wire or along bamboo canes if you prefer, nailed to pegs driven into the soil; and when this rod has reached a length of thirteen feet, you bend the end of it downwards and push it firmly to a depth of six inches or more into the ground. It will then take root (we hope), and will spring up quite soon in new growth for the next rod, when you repeat the process, over and over again until your original vine with its recurrent progeny has attained the length you require.

You see the advantages. First, you need only one rootstock to start the process; very economical. (Of course, if you like to plant two, one at either end, it would go quicker, and they would meet in the middle, like engineers working through an Alpine tunnel.) Secondly, you can control your rods into any shape to suit the layout of your garden; you could grow them in a straight line down a long path, for example, or you could make them turn sharp corners at

E

right angles to form an enclosure, vines being very flexible and tractable. Thirdly, by the time the rods have made old wood they should need no propping or staking; they will have grown tough enough to support themselves. Fourthly, you can, if you wish, grow this serialized vine a mile long. What a thought! Fifthly, you can eat the grapes.

Finally, you can buy or borrow Mr. Hyams's book, where you will find far more detailed instructions than I have space to reproduce here.

April 27, 1952

A public activity is afoot which is bound to have a very considerable effect upon the future appearance of our country. I refer to the schemes for tree and hedge planting both in urban areas and along roads and by-passes. It is satisfactory to reflect that while on the one hand we are busy destroying our woodlands and our hedgerow timber, on the other hand a watchful Ministry is issuing leaflets for the guidance of local authorities and committees; leaflets which, on the whole, are sensibly and even imaginatively composed, with an eye to what Government departments will insist upon calling amenity value, but which we in our simplicity still obstinately call beauty.

It is encouraging to find that, apart from such obvious recommendations as the plane, the birch, the lime, the ash, the sycamore, the horse-chestnut, the beech and the poplar, including the sweet-scented balsam poplar, due consideration has also been given to the wild cherry, or gean, that bride of spring; to the whitebeam, whose under-leaf blows silver in the breeze; to the tulip tree, with its strange green-and-yellow flowers; to the catalpa, whose flowers seem a mixture between the spotted foxglove and a miniature orchid; to the ginkgo, or maidenhair tree; and to the robinias, or false acacias, with special mention for the pale-pink variety, *Decaisneana,* so much less familiar than the white.

All these proposals show more appreciation and imagination than we are accustomed to associate with an office desk in Whitehall. Perusing Circular No. 24, we note also with delighted approval that autumn colouring has been remembered, and that the wild service tree finds a place with its bright gold, as well as the sweet gum, whose botanical name is for once far more descriptive: *Liquidambar.*

It is only when we come to what most people regard as the relatively small flowering trees, with that dangerous adjective *ornamental* attached to them, that our confidence begins to wobble. It is so easy, and so delusive, to become excited over a new introduction when first you see it. The sight of the golden rain of the laburnum must have been as intoxicating to our Victorian forebears as their glass of champagne poured out on rare occasions. Yet to-day, the laburnum suffers from 'cheap' associations. It retains its original beauty; but has become too common, too ubiquitous, to provide us with the pleasure of surprise.

We should not, I think, maintain too horticulturally snobbish an attitude towards such things. Ubiquity should not necessarily affect beauty, properly used. Yet at the same time I would like to suggest that what is commonly known as 'an eye-full' does not always survive the test of years. Popular taste, easily caught, quickly turns into bad taste; or, at any rate, into a taste rejected by the more fastidious. We do not want to see our new roads and council sites planted with the screaming pink that once caught our raw fancy.

I observe, for instance, with regret, that a variety of the Japanese flowering-cherry known as *Hisakura* is given an "esp." mark of commendation. Why? If the Ministry means the true *Hisakura,* well and good, but I suspect that what the local authorities will in fact obtain is that wickedly vulgar *Kansan*, so strong and crude that it will spread like measles in an infectious rash.

Let us drop from this high temperature to a cooler degree. Let us consider the less garish flowering trees, which should survive the test of taste and time better than the 'eye-fulls.' The Ministry rightly recommends the common almond, and some of the Japanese cherries such as *Yedoensis*, *Sargentii*, and *Lannesiana erecta*, which, with its fastigiate or poplar-like habit, seems particularly well adapted to roadside planting. But no mention is made of other even more subtly beautiful varieties such as *Tai-Hoku*, the great white cherry; or the greenish *Ukon*; or the hill cherry, an object of inspiration in Japan; or of the snowy mespilus, *Amelanchier canadensis*.

It may be argued that the general public prefer the bright pinks—'So cheerful'—and that the proof is to be found in a myriad suburban gardens; but this private planting should suffice without the encouragement of reinforcements supplied from the municipal purse. It is, we submit, the duty of Governmental advisers gently to decoy the public taste (and the taste of local councils) into more desirable channels.

It is already apparent that somebody in Whitehall knows a great deal of what he is talking about: could he not go a step further and empanel some of our great gardeners, amateur and professional, in an extra-advisory capacity? In this country of gardens and garden-lovers the opportunity has never been greater; it would be a sad pity if our roads and open spaces, our new towns, our housing estates, were now to be filled officially with a type of planting analogous, in terms of trees, to the begonias and calceolarias of many a public garden.

May

May 6, 1951

THERE was once a man, it is said, who furnished his garden entirely with the wild flowers of Britain. He was not one of those well-intentioned vandals who dig up a plant with no knowledge of how or when to transplant it; who have no regard for the conditions in which it would wish to be replanted; and who then turn plaintively indignant when it dies. For such people there is no excuse save the excuse of ignorance, which is the worst of all. This man knew what he was about, and no doubt was responsible for saving many things that might otherwise have perished.

In these days there is ample justification for such judicious rescues. Our native flowers are threatened. Intensive agriculture has ploughed up many an acre of the Lent-lily, the cowslip, and the orchid. Tree-felling has trampled many a wood where the lily-of-the-valley once flourished. Clearance of ditches has buried many a thriving violet under mounds of soggy earth. (I am happy to say that I retrieved masses of wild white violets when I noticed that this fate was about to overtake them; they are now safe in my garden.) All this effort towards better agriculture was, and is, of course, necessary, but other horrible ideas now menace our wild flowers. Report suggests that selective weed-killers are to be used, or perhaps are already being used, on the grass verges of our lanes. This will mean the disappearance of many graceful things such as the Meadow-sweet, the wild strawberry, the Lords-and-Ladies, the Lady's smock . . . all innocents, no match for the abominable ingenuity of man.

What can be done about it? How can we combat this chemical destruction? I wish that someone, perhaps a reader of this article, would write a practical pamphlet about the salvation of our wild flowers, advising us how to mark a plant for its seed at the ripening season; how to mark a bulb or a root for lifting at the right time; how to save, in fact, our native treasures which the selective weed-killer will, with its wicked efficiency, regard merely as weeds.

For those readers especially interested in the survival of our native orchids, I would like to recommend *Wild Orchids of Britain*, by V. S. Summerhayes (Collins, 21s., illustrated). Mr. Summerhayes is the Kew Gardens authority on orchids, so you may take it that his word is to be believed. He gives some useful maps as an appendix to his book, showing where our native orchids are mostly to be found. It is exciting to see an outline map of Britain, blocked out in black, area by area, county by county, where these rarities occur. The maps alone should be enough to send orchid hunters out on the quest; and the text will certainly ensure a respectful care.

May 13, 1951

There is a race of little irises, flowering in April and May, too seldom grown. They do not aspire to make a great splash; their colours are frail; they grow only six to twelve inches high; they demand a small place to match their small size; they must be regarded as intimate flowers, to be peered into and protected from the vulgar slug. I am referring to miniature versions of the Bearded Iris, which is the sort most familiar to most people. These miniature versions are called *pumila* and *chamaeiris*.

I will not waste space quarrelling over botanical differences. I will say only that if you can buy what nursery-men usually term *Iris pumila* you will get a reward. There is *I. azurea*, and *I. coerulea*, and *I. lutea*, a yellow one. They cost about 1s. 6d. each. Having paid this price, where is it best to plant them?

The authorities seem to differ in their opinion. W. R. Dykes, who was the great authority on irises, says that *Iris pumila* ought to be divided and transplanted every second year. He says they exhaust the soil. Yet I have grown a patch of them in a stone sink for some ten years and they have never flowered better than this year. The behaviour of plants is indeed inexplicable. It breaks all the rules; and that is what makes gardening so endlessly various and interesting.

I have come to the conclusion, after many years of some-times sad experience, that you cannot come to any con-clusion at all. But one simple thing I have discovered in gardening; a simple thing one never sees mentioned in gardening books. It is the fact that many plants do better if they can get their roots under stones. This is a fact I would like to return to in a future article. In the mean-time, since I set out to mention the little early irises, may I suggest that you might plant them into the cracks between paving or along the edges of a paved path, where they will not be walked on? I feel sure that this is the place to grow them, rather than down the front of a border, as is often recommended in books about gardening. They are not things for an herbaceous border: they are things for stone paths, surely; and the grey background of the paving enhances their delicacy of colouring. The worst that can be said against them is that they do not remain very long in flower, but they are so unobtrusive and take up so little room, that their few weeks of flowering life entitle them to a place where they can subsequently grow forgotten.

May 20, 1951

There is often a strip of ground in a garden which cannot be put to good purpose without more labour than we can devote to it. It may once have been a lawn, which means mowing; or a long border, which needs weeding and upkeep; or merely a strip along the boundary fence in the garden of a new house, hitherto uncultivated, which demands some treatment to turn it into something better than a rough waste. I had an idea for such a place, which should be both pretty and labour-saving.

The shape does not matter so very much; it could be rectangular, square, or even circular, though I fancy a long narrow rectangle would give the best effect. What is important is that it should be *flat*, and that the ground surface should be level. No bumps: no depressions. You then plant it at regular intervals (say fifteen feet apart either way) with young stripling sapling trees, straight of stem and twiggy of head; it will be important to keep the stems clean of growth so that you can always see through and between them. A thin little grove is what I have in mind. The silver birch with its pale bark would be ideal, especially in a light or sandy soil; the lime or linden, for any soil; the whitebeam, whose underside leaves show silver in the breeze; and even young oaks, round-topped and grown as standards.

The question will then arise of what you plant underneath. Since the heads of the little trees will be very green, the accent should be on emphasizing the greenness. Turf is probably impossible, because of the mowing, and anyway I think one should aim at a brighter green than that. I have a great weakness for Sweet Woodruff; it does not object to shade, it remains green from April until the autumn, it can be grown from seed, and it would make a dense cushion rather like those enormous eiderdowns (*duvets*) that one finds in old-fashioned French hotels. I

would also plant some patches of greenish flowers; for
instance, the green and silver Star-of-Bethlehem, *Orni-
thogalum nutans*; our native wood anemone; lily of the
valley; and, for later in the year, some clumps of Solomon's
Seal and the sweet-smelling *Smilacina racemosa*. I am not
quite sure about these last two: they might be too tall,
and might interrupt the vistas between the straight little
trunks. Obviously such planting must depend upon individual taste, but of one thing I feel sure: that all colour
must be excluded. It must all be green and white; cool,
symmetrical, and severe.

May 27, 1951

May I go back to something I wrote a couple of weeks
ago about many plants doing so well if they can get their
roots under stones? I am not thinking specially of Alpines
whose natural habit it is, but of casual strays, often self-
sown, sometimes bulbous plants, sometimes merely annuals
or biennials, which by a successful accident have pointed
the way to this method of gardening. The narrowest crack
in a path or paved terrace will surprisingly send up the
finest seedling; I have known even such large unwanted
subjects as delphiniums and hollyhocks to make the attempt.
The reason, obviously, is that they never suffer from either
excessive moisture or excessive drought; the stone preserves
such moisture as is in the soil, but prevents the soggy pud-
dling consequent on a heavy rainfall; furthermore, it protects
from the scorching sun and consequent wilting which
demands the watering-can.

If we are to take this hint from Nature it would be as
well to dispose of the weeds first to save trouble later on.
Weeds in paths are a constant worry to those who have not
discovered the ghoulish pleasure of using weed-killer; and,
even to the initiate, the cost of proprietary weed-killers
is often a deterrent, driving many a conscientious gardener

back to the kneeling-pad and the broken knife-blade. It is now possible, however, to buy sodium chlorate by the pound; the price fluctuates so I had better not quote it, but as you must use only 1 lb. to 10 gallons of water you can see that it works out very cheaply. Sodium chlorate acts through the leaves, so should be applied when the weeds are green—the only drawback is that the ground is not safe to set other plants in for about six months.

I should then fill up the cracks with good soil or compost, and sow quite recklessly. I should not mind how ordinary my candidates were, Royal Blue forget-me-not, pansies, wallflowers, Indian pinks, alyssum Violet Queen, because I should pull up 95 per cent later on, leaving only single specimens here and there. It is not, after all, a flower-bed that we are trying to create. If, however, you think it is a waste of opportunity to sow such ordinary things, there are plenty of low-growing plants of a choicer kind, especially those which dislike excessive damp at the root throughout the winter: this covering of stone would protect them from that. The old-fashioned pinks would make charming tufts: *Dad's favourite*, or *Inchmery*, or *Little Jock*, or *Susan*, or *Thomas*. The Allwoodii, with their suggestion of chintz and of patchwork quilts, should also succeed under such conditions; I confess to repeated failures with them in open borders, but their neatness and variety encourage perseverance

May 4, 1952

There must be some curious philological or Grimm's Law which makes English-speaking people call anemones anenomes, transferring the *m* into the place of the *n*. So perhaps it is better to adopt the pretty though unscientific name of Wind-flower, as it is about the anemones or wind-flowers that I want to write on this day of spring.

How gay they are, how brilliantly gay, how shiny, how variegated in their colours, these wind-flowers that come to us from different parts of the world. The season starts for us from Greece, with the starry blue *Anemone blanda* flowering in March; succeeded by *A. Apennina*, the equally starry and even more intensely blue Italian. Then there is the well-known double or semi-double *St. Brigid*, on sale everywhere early in the year, but to my mind greatly excelled by the *de Caen*, or poppy-flowered single; and excelled above all by the single, starry, *St. Bavo*. This is the one I ardently want to commend to your attention at the moment.

I cannot imagine why people don't grow *Anemone St. Bavo* more generously. It is cheap to buy, 2s. 6d. a dozen of those little tubers which one doesn't know which way up to plant and it doesn't seem to matter anyhow—English as she is wrote. *St. Bavo* is a hybrid of *Anemone coronaria*, and comes up in a range of colouring equalled by very few other easy flowers. Any description of the various colours would sound, on paper, like an exaggeration: wine-velvet with an electric-blue centre; scarlet with a black centre, pink or lilac with a biscuit-coloured centre; or a particularly subtle named variety, more expensive at 6s. 6d. a dozen, called *Salmonea*, which is like a ripe apricot hanging in the sun. At least, I thought it was, but when with a conscientious qualm I went back to have another look at it, I found I had been quite wrong. It was more as though you had pounded some old Tudor bricks into a paste, varnished the paste, and then shredded it into pointed petals.

May 11, 1952

Often I receive plaintive appeals from gardeners who live in towns, or from gardeners whose site is heavily shaded, or from gardeners whose lot is cast in a combination of both. I never quite know what to reply, having no personal knowledge of such conditions, and being reluctant to proffer advice unsupported by practical experience. In

common with everyone else, I know, roughly, that Morello
cherries and the winter Jasmine will flourish on a North
wall, and that periwinkles and foxgloves and ferns will
tolerate a considerable amount of shade, but very soon after
that I find myself coming to a full stop.

It was therefore with relief that I welcomed a little
pamphlet called *Plants for the Shaded Garden,* by Barbara
Acworth, published by the University of London Press at
the modest price of 1s. 6d. Obviously, it would be unreason-
able to demand a comprehensive treatise for eighteenpence,
or to expect anything likely to tell the advanced, progressive
gardener something he did not already know. I do feel,
however, that I can confidently recommend this cheapest
of all gardening books (most of them cost from 10s. 6d.
to a guinea) to the amateur gardener struggling to
make his patch of prettiness or beauty in unpropitious
circumstances.

I noticed with particular pleasure that Miss Acworth hit
on some favourites of mine: Sweet Woodruff, for example,
Asperula odorata, which consents to make a broad green
band of edging in deep shade, starred with tiny white
flowers just now, in May. This is a native of Britain, much
neglected; I have often tried to bring it into favour, and
am glad to receive Miss Acworth's support. Altogether this
is a most helpful and discriminating little book, with
sensible notes of instruction to each plant mentioned. I
cannot help suspecting, however, that something funny has
happened on page 19 to the description of *Vitis heterophylla,*
which is made to resemble what we usually call Virginia
creeper. *Vitis heterophylla* is not self clinging, as Miss
Acworth states, nor does it turn crimson in autumn. Its
claim to distinction lies in its china-blue berries. And if she
wanted to call the Virginia creeper a vine at all, should
she not have written *Vitis inconstans*?

May 18, 1952

The happy few who still maintain a greenhouse, however small, sufficiently warmed in winter to keep the frost out, will find themselves repaid if they can make room for a few pots of the unfamiliar, pretty, blue-flowered *Oxypetalum caeruleum.** This, admittedly, is subtle rather than showy, but I notice that it always attracts attention when we stand the pots out of doors for the summer in the garden. It has downy-green leaves and flowers of a curious greyish-blue, with a bright blue button no bigger than a flattened seed-pearl in the middle. I like to associate it with some pots of *Plumbago capensis,* whose stronger blue marries into a mist of blues reinforcing one another. Both, of course, are cool greenhouse plants, but they will live very happily in the open from the end of May until October.

I like the habit of pot gardening. It reminds me of the South—Italy, Spain, Provence, where pots of carnations and zinnias are stood carelessly about, in a sunny courtyard or rising in tiers on the treads of an outside stair, dusty but oh how gay! I know it entails constant watering, but consider the convenience of being able to set down a smear of colour just where you need it, in some corner where an earlier flower has gone off. We should take this hint from other lands. We do not make nearly enough use of pots in our country, partly, I suspect, because we have no tradition of pot-making here, nothing to compare with the camellia-pot, a common thing in Italy, swagged with garlands looped from a lion's mouth. Several times have I tried to persuade brick-makers to reproduce this standardized Italian model. They look at it with suspicion and alarm. 'Oh, no, we couldn't do that. We have never done anything like that. Sorry, we can't oblige.'

Meanwhile we surround a huge black Chinese jar

* *Oxypetalum caeruleum* is now known as *Tweedia caerutea,* or *Amblyopetalum caeruleum.* It is a native of Brazil.

with the blue *Oxypetalum* and the blue plumbago all through the summer, and drop a potful of *Ipomea rubro-caerulea* (Morning Glory, Heavenly Blue) into the Chinese jar, to pour downwards into a symphony of different blues.

The Chinese jar is of romantic origin. It was made during the Ming dynasty, which might mean anything between 1368 and 1644—and was used to transport porcelain from China to Egypt, packed in lard to keep it from rattling about. The very solid handles show where the ropes were passed through, to sling it on board ship. It is not really black, but a sort of aubergine colour.

May 25, 1952

The flowering shrubs and trees are full of especial richness this year, from the common hawthorn in the hedgerows to the treasured beauties in our gardens. They are over all too soon, and it is then, as they begin to fade, that we regret not having kept a record of them in their prime, with a view to possible rearrangements, alterations, eliminations or additions when planting time comes in the autumn. One thinks one will remember, but, in fact, the succession is so rapid and one picture is so quickly replaced by another picture, that our impressions become merged into a blur of colours, shapes, sizes, and seasons. Why, we cry too late, did we not take notes week by week at the time?

It is with a virtuous resolution that I have acquired a large note-book stamped GARDEN RECORDS and four bundles of inch-long labels, with gilt numerals incised on white, from 1 to 100. These, since they are each pierced with a little hole, can be tied to a branch and the corresponding description entered against the number in the note-book. Thus: 'No. 10. Shockingly poor washy lilac; destroy; and replace by No. 12.' A reference to No. 12 recalls that it is 'Fine double-red young lilac; deserves a

better place.' There comes a moment in the history of every
garden when the duds must be scrapped, and the ill-assorted
companions separated. My little outfit, supplied by Messrs.
Woodman, High Street, Pinner, is by far the most con-
venient register of such ruthless intentions of future
discipline.

A genus of small shrubs which I fancy would never
require a removal ticket are the Deutzias. Graceful and
arching, May–June flowerers, four to six feet, they are ideal
for the small garden where space is a consideration. They
are easy, not even resenting a little lime in the soil, but
beware of pruning them if you do not wish to lose the
next year's bloom. The most you should do is to cut off
the faded sprays and, naturally, take out any dead wood.
The only thing to be said against them is that a late frost
will damage the flower, and that is a risk which can well
be taken. *Deutzia gracilis rosea*, rosy as its name implies;
D. pulchra, white; *D. scabra Pride of Rochester*, pinkish
white, rather taller, should make a pretty group. They are
not very expensive at 3s. 6d. to 4s. 6d.

June

June 3, 1951

'DOING the flowers.' This douce and dulcet though lengthy task has been facilitated for us by Constance Spry, whose ingenuity is boundless. Nothing comes amiss to her in the exercise of her art, whether it be a sheaf of purple roses, or a leaf of red cabbage, or a spray of ripe blackberries, cut from the hedgerow. Her latest book, *Summer and Autumn Flowers* (Dent, 21s.), is full of suggestions, and is to be followed by a second volume called *Winter and Spring Flowers*.

I have not the pleasure of knowing Mrs. Spry personally,* but I can see that we would agree; we would click; we would say 'Oh, yes,' and 'Oh, no,' in the enthusiastic way that gardeners have of concurring over the things they value. Mrs. Spry must have a large garden of her own, where she cultivates plants for her own pleasure as well as for her celebrated shop in London, but there is nothing necessarily extravagant about her methods; it is true that she can avail herself of an armful of lilies and mix them with *Humea elegans* in a golden urn, but she is equally happy with fir-cones or with some of the ordinary herbs such as fennel, whose lovely feathery foliage has not escaped her eye, or with the yellow heads of the Woad that once furnished our ancestors with a blue dye. The receptacles into which she puts her flowers are equally

* I had not then; I have now.

varied: a wooden bowl, a silver sauce-boat, a tin-lined
Bible-box, and something which she calls a pancheon.

Not the least useful part of her book is the section which
deals with the care of cut flowers. As most of us already
know, flowers last very much longer if you have previously
stamped on their stems, stripped them of their leaves, and
plunged them into boiling water. Detailed instructions are
given as to which flowers respond best to this medieval-
sounding treatment.

June 10, 1951

Visitors to the Chelsea Show may have noticed a large
platform or billiard-table entirely planted with *Gentiana
acaulis*. Billiard-tables are usually green, but this one was
blue. The deep yet brilliant colour of those trumpets, raised
motionless in a fanfare of blue music, must have aroused
envy in many hearts.

Perhaps one should hesitate to recommend so temperamental a plant. It is said, for instance, that *G. acaulis* will
flower freely on one side of a path but not on the other,
for no apparent reason; and certainly the advice given by
successful growers is bewildering in its variety. Reginald
Farrer believed in a rich diet; feed it, he said, on old boots,
pig-trough garbage, and the blood of kings. Other people
will tell you to stamp on it; others, again, that where a
particular little cress-like weed flourishes, there also will
the gentian thrive. Two things seem certain: that it dislikes
drought at the roots, taking the usual revenge if you allow
it to get parched; and that you must try it in different
places until you find the right place. I have had three shots
at it myself, and at last it seems pleased, though I cannot
yet rival the gentleman who replied modestly to Farrer's
inquiry by saying that he 'did not think he had much more
than five miles of it.' A statement which, upon investigation,
turned out to be true.

F

82 IN YOUR GARDEN AGAIN

For the comfort of gardeners on an alkaline soil, it may
be added that *G. acaulis* is a lime-lover, unlike the
September-flowering gentian *sino-ornata*, which dies instantly at one distant sniff of lime. Mortar-rubble, with its
natural content of a lot of lime, and a top-dressing of bone
meal are both gratefully received by *G. acaulis*. And for
the further comfort of gardeners who want a patch of
gentians, not necessarily five miles long, in their garden,
and who want to depend on an August display, *Gentiana
septemfida* is probably the best and easiest to grow.
Septemfida, by the way, has nothing to do with September,
although it sounds like it; 'septemfida' merely means
'cleaved into seven divisions.' This gentian wants a peaty,
loamy, leaf-mouldy bed; and hates getting parched.

If you want to know more about this beautiful family,
a work on gentians has recently been published: *Gentians*,
by David Wilkie, Country Life, 25s., generously illustrated
with photographs.

June 17, 1951

Mr. William Robinson, in his classic work *The English
Flower Garden*, was very scornful of the Alliums or ornamental garlics. He said that they were 'not of much value
in the garden'; that they produced so many little bulblets
as to make themselves too numerous; and that they smelt
when crushed.

For once, I must disagree with that eminent authority.
I think, on the contrary, that some of the Alliums have
a high value in the June garden; far from objecting to a
desirable plant making a spreading nuisance of itself, I am
only too thankful that it should do so; and as for smelling
nasty when crushed—well, who in his senses would wish
wantonly to crush his own flowers?

Allium Rosenbachianum is extremely handsome, four feet
tall, with big, rounded lilac heads delicately touched with

green. Its leaves, however, are far from handsome, so it
should be planted behind something which will conceal
them. If you are by nature a hoarder, you can cut down
the long stems after the flowers have faded and keep them
with their seed-pods for what is known to florists as 'interior
decoration' throughout the winter. Like most of the garlics,
they demand a sunny, well-drained situation. Not expensive
at 5s. 6d. a dozen, for the effect they produce, they get
better and better after the first year of planting.

Allium albo-pilosum, a Persian, my favourite, is lilac in
colour, two feet high or so. (See also under June 29, 1952.)
Allium cyaneum is a mite, four inches only, blue, suitable
for sinks or troughs, or any place where it can be observed
at eye-level. The white-headed garlic, *Allium neapolitanum*,
is useful for cutting; is apparently indestructible; and is
cheap at 2s. 6d. a dozen bulbs.

Allium giganteum, five feet tall, is generally agreed to
be the grandest of all, but is also the most expensive at
6s. a bulb. I bought a single one last year, and am now
watching it anxiously. It should flower in July.

Mr. Ralph Cusack, whose address will be found on
p.175, is an Allium enthusiast and offers a grand list of
varieties in his catalogue.

June 24, 1951

We all have associations with the familiar scents of our
childhood, whether they be of sweet-briar on a moist
evening, or of a red rose warmed by the sun, or of our
native honeysuckle threading its way through a hedge. It
is thus rather a shock to find some honeysuckles which
have no scent at all, but which have flowers of such
surprising beauty that they are worth growing for their
colour alone.

Some of these are now flowering in my garden. I like
and admire them, though I cannot love them in the way

one loves the old sentimental kinds which always smelt so good. The ones with the huge yellow scentless flowers are called *Lonicera Tellmaniana* and *Lonicera tragophylla*. There is also a bright red-orange one, *Lonicera Brownii fuchsioides*. They seem to do well in sun or shade; trained against a wall, or scrambling over a fence. I never know whether I prefer them in sun or in shade. The sunshine paints a brilliance on them, with a varnishing brush of light; but in a shady corner they have the deep, secret glow of hidden things.

I have recently regretted that I did not plant more honeysuckles in my garden. I suppose that all gardeners are suddenly assailed by similar pangs of regret. Fortunately, in the case of the honeysuckles, which are fast-growing subjects, it is an omission which can be rectified this coming autumn. For the scented ones, I shall plant the Early Dutch, flowering in May and June: and the late Dutch, flowering from July to September or October. These are both related to our native honeysuckle. For winter flowering, I have already got *Lonicera fragrantissima* and its perhaps better fellow, *Lonicera Standishii*. They do not flower very exuberantly, in my experience, but even a couple of sprays picked in January are welcome and will scent a whole room.

June 1, 1952

New York, so we are told, could not spread sideways beyond a certain area owing to the geological formations on which that astonishing city has arisen. It had to go vertically towards the sky because it could not spread horizontally across the land. This curious and interesting fact accounts for that most original form of architecture, the skyscraper. No one had even thought of building skyscrapers before, because there was no need to. There had always been plenty of ground-room.

Now in small gardens there is not always as much
ground-room as the gardener greedily wants, and I saw
recently in the relatively small garden of a friend a most
ingenious idea for getting herself out of the cramped difficulty. She had been given a flat flower-bed to deal with, but
instead of leaving it just flat and restricted in space, she
had built it up into little terraces with rough stones; three
stories high, and into these little stone-walled terraces she
had packed and crammed every kind of plant that enjoys
good drainage conditions: pinks, thrift, campanulas,
Lewisias, violas, all ordinary things, but so effective grown
in tiers as she was growing them, in a foaming mass and
fall of flower and colour. You see the idea? You get the
benefit three ways. You get the stone-walling, you get the
flat bits under the stone-walling, and then on the top you
get a wide expanse of bed in which you can plant anything
you like. You will, by this means, have increased your
garden space threefold.

Apart from the gain in space, it is always amusing to
try experiments with plants in a dry-wall, even though
that wall may not be more than two stones high. Many
plants will flourish which otherwise would perish from the
damp of our climate. When they can get their roots back
between stones they seem to tuck themselves in and
preserve themselves from rot. We do not need to build
a skyscraper: we need only two rows of stone to pack our
native Cheddar Pink into, let us say, or some of the
Allwoodii pinks which sometimes prove disappointing
grown in an ordinary border.

June 8, 1952

There is a form of hypocrisy common to nearly all
gardeners. It does not affect only the gentle amateur, but
has been known to affect even the most hardened professional, who is not, generally speaking, a sentimental or

squeamish man. It is the human weakness which, accompanying our determination to rid ourselves of our slugs and snails, makes us reluctant next morning to contemplate the result of our over-night efforts.

Having enjoyed our own good breakfast, we come out to behold the slimy greenish remains. Big black slugs, four inches long; little black slugs, one inch long; snails exuding their entrails from under their beautiful delicate shells. . . . Meta-and-sawdust have done their work only too well. In what agony, during the dark hours, have these miserable members of God's Creation perished? We ordained it, knowing, nay, hoping for what would happen; but when we see it we do not like it. We remember the lyrical terms in which the poets have addressed our victims:

> To note on hedgerow baulks, in moisture sprent,
>   The jetty snail creep from the mossy thorn,
> With earnest heed, and tremulous intent,
>   Frail brother of the morn!

Shakespeare also had a flattering comparison for him:

> Love's feeling is more soft and sensible
> Than are the tender horns of cockled snails.

It is all very painful, unpleasant, and even nauseating. What is to be done about it? We must abolish our frail brother with his tender horns, or else sacrifice our seedlings: we have the choice. The seedlings, I think, will win; must win. We must kill their enemies, but, if we are humane in our hearts, we will commit this slaughter with the least distressing offence to our hypocritical selves.

I think I have found the answer in an anti-slug bait which causes slugs and snails to shrivel up, dryly. It really works: I have tried it. It is called Anti-slug, and it comes from Messrs. Baker, Codsall, Wolverhampton. It is said to be harmless to plants, birds and animals. And all I hope

is that it doesn't cause unnecessary suffering to those
humble enemies who creep across our paths, and have to
be destroyed.

June 15, 1952

Brave gardeners who have a sunny corner to spare, at
the foot of a south wall for choice, and a poor sandy soil,
should plant some bulbs of Ixia, the South African Corn-lily.
It is a graceful thing, about eighteen inches high, with
rush-like leaves and a flower-spike in various colours: white,
yellow, coral-pink, and sometimes striped like the boiled
sweets of our childhood. These, in a mixture, cost about
2s. 6d. a dozen, or 17s. 6d. a hundred. There is also a
particularly lovely and rather strange variety, green with
a black centre, *Ixia viridiflora*, more expensive at 12s. 6d.
a dozen.

Ixias are not entirely hardy, though hardier than the
freesias which they somewhat resemble. Very sharp
drainage, deep planting of about six inches, and a little
cover throughout our damp winter, should, however,
ensure their survival, and those which fail to reappear can
be replaced annually for half a crown. Of course, the more
you can plant, the better. They flower in June and take
up very little room. They are ideal for picking, as they
last a long time in water and arrange themselves with thin
and slender elegance in a tall glass.

They do also very well as pot-plants in a cold greenhouse
or a conservatory, not requiring any heat but only protection from frost. If you grow them this way, you must
disregard the advice to plant them six inches deep, and
cover them with only an inch or so of soil—sandy loam
and a handful of leaf-mould mixed to each pot, and crocks
for drainage at the bottom.

I do hope you will order some Ixias for planting next
October or November. I admit that they are apt to die out

after a year or so; but to those gardeners who have a poor, starved soil and a warm corner they are a God-given present in June.

June 22, 1952

Often one is asked for plants which will flourish in semi-shade, and in the month of June the noble peony comes to mind. (I mean the herbaceous sort, not the species or the Tree-peony.) It always seems to me that the herbaceous peony is the very epitome of June. Larger than any rose, it has something of the cabbage rose's voluminous quality; and when it finally drops from the vase, it sheds its vast petticoats with a bump on the table, all in an intact heap, much as a rose will suddenly fall, making us look up from our book or conversation, to notice for one moment the death of what had still appeared to be a living beauty.

To be practical, there is much to recommend the peony. I will make a list of its virtues. It is a very long-lived plant, increasing yearly in vigour if you will only leave it undisturbed. It likes to stay put. It will, as I said, flourish in half-shade, and indeed its brag of size and colour gains from the broken light of overhanging branches. It doesn't object to an alkaline soil, a great advantage to those who cannot grow lime-hating plants in their garden. Rabbits do not appear to care for its young shoots. Slugs don't care for it either; and the only disease it may seriously suffer from is *wilt*, a fungus, *Botrytis*. If this appears, you must cut out the diseased bits and burn them; but in the many years I have grown peonies in my garden I have, touch wood, never found any trace of disease amongst my gross Edwardian swagger ladies.

The secret of growing the herbaceous peonies is to plant them very shallow and give them a deep, rich root-run of manure for their roots to find as they go down in search of nourishment. Then they will go ahead, and probably outlive the person who planted them, so that his or her grandchild will be picking finer flowers fifty years hence.

June 29, 1952

I know a man who collects baths. He buys broken-down baths for a few shillings at local auction sales and buries them in his garden, with the waste-hole open and a thick layer of coke-clinker or some similar rough stuff underneath to ensure drainage. He then fills the bath up to the rim with whatever kind of soil he requires; covers the rim over to hide it; and there he is, with a securely insulated patch in which to grow his choosy plants.

I am not suggesting that our gardens should all become a submerged cemetery for obsolete baths, but it does seem to me a helpful idea for people who have a difficult soil to cope with—people who want to grow things that will not consent to flourish in the soil with which they have been blessed or cursed. The dwellers on chalk, for example, who wish to grow the lime-hating gentians, could overcome their difficulty. The dwellers on clay would find that the indestructible, uncontrollable clay could be eliminated in favour of a soft bed suitable to peat-loving subjects. Again, if you want a swampy bit of ground for moisture-loving primulas, you can create it, very suitably, in the buried bath. Again, if you have a flinty soil, which throws up flints over and over again from the bottom, however often you may think you have cleared them out, you can replace that spiteful bit of ground with a richer loam, controlled and contained within the rectangular shape of the sunken bath.

It is an idea lending itself to much expansion.

Meanwhile I have been deriving much pleasure from a June-flowering garlic called *Allium albo-pilosum*. A native of Turkestan, it comes up in a large mop-sized head of numerous perfectly star-shaped flowers of sheeny lilac, each with a little green button at the centre, on long thin stalks, so that the general effect is of a vast mauve-and-green cobweb, quivering with its own lightness and buoyancy. They can be bought for 5s. a dozen, but even a group of six makes a fine show. Quite easy to grow, they prefer a light soil and a sunny place, and may be increased to any extent by the little bulbils which form round the parent bulb, a most economical way of multiplying your stock. They would mix very happily with the blue *Allium azureum*, sometimes called *A. caeruleum*, in front of them. These cost only 2s. 9d. a dozen, are not quite so tall, and overlap in their flowering season, thus prolonging the display.

July

I AM astonished, and even alarmed, by the growth which
certain roses will make in the course of a few years.
There is one called *Madame Plantier*, which we planted
at the foot of a worthless old apple tree, vaguely hoping
that it might cover a few feet of the trunk. Now it is 15 feet
high with a girth of 15 yards, tapering towards the top
like the waist of a Victorian beauty and pouring down in
a vast crinoline stitched all over with its white sweet-scented
clusters of flower.

Madame Plantier dates back, in fact, to 1835, just two
years before Queen Victoria came to the throne, so she and
the Queen may be said to have grown up together towards
the crinolines of their maturity. Queen Victoria is dead,
but *Madame Plantier* still very much alive. I go out to
look at her in the moonlight: she gleams, a pear-shaped
ghost, contriving to look both matronly and virginal. She
has to be tied up round her tree, in long strands, otherwise
she would make only a big straggly bush; we have found
that the best method is to fix a sort of tripod of bean-poles
against the tree and tie the strands to that.

Another favourite white rose of mine is *Paul's Lemon
Pillar*. It should not be called white. A painter might see
it as greenish, suffused with sulphur-yellow, and its great
merit lies not only in the vigour of its growth and wealth
of flowering, but also in the perfection of its form. The
shapeliness of each bud has a sculptural quality which

suggests curled shavings of marble, if one may imagine
marble made of the softest ivory suede. The full-grown
flower is scarcely less beautiful; and when the first explosion
of bloom is over, a carpet of thick white petals covers the
ground, so dense as to look as though it had been deliberately
laid.

The old *Madame Alfred Carrière* is likewise in full flower.
Smaller than Paul's rose, and with no pretensions to a
marmoreal shape, *Madame Alfred*, white, flushed with
shell-pink, has the advantage of a sweet, true-rose scent,
and will grow to the eaves of any reasonably proportioned
house, even on a west or north wall. I should like to see
every Airey house in this country rendered invisible behind
this curtain of white and green.

July 8, 1951

One of these days I must cope with what once tried to
be an herbaceous border, but which is now a mess and a
compromise. Herbaceous borders, perhaps, have had their
day. They require to be immaculately kept and elaborately
planned if they are to give their best; no pleasure can be
derived from a jumble of plants, stuck in irrespective of
colour or character, flopping after rain, prostrate after a
sudden gale, tousled, sodden, leaning sideways at all
angles, delphiniums in the back row, lupins and phlox
in the middle, catmint and pinks along the front . . .
one is only too familiar with these survivals of Edwardian
times.

The question of staking is always a difficult one. Twiggy
peasticks, pushed in at an early stage of the growth, are
preferable to a stockade of bamboos hastily added as an
afterthought when heads become top-heavy: peasticks will
be hidden and covered over, as bamboos never will. I was
told recently of an ingenious method for supporting perennial subjects in the border. In the idle, indoor days of winter

you employ your leisure making large circles of stout wire, criss-crossing them with thinner wire into, say, four sections, meeting in a sort of hub at the middle; you then supply a central pole, of metal if you can get it, say bits of an old area railing, more durable than wood. In the spring you start your wire circle a few inches from the ground, raising it gradually up the central pole as the height of the plant increases, and as the plant grows up through the sections. I thought to myself that one might improve on the idea by placing two or more of the wire circles round the pole, according to the eventual height expected of the plant; this would save keeping a constant watch to see if the circle needed raising, and would also afford a double support to brittle stems.

It would entail a good deal of winter work, neat fingers, a pair of wire-cutters, a pair of pincers, and a couple of rolls of wire, thick and thin; but you would then have a fixture to last without renewal for many years. Even if you have not got an herbaceous border properly speaking, it should be a useful hint applied to any special treasure of a plant, too snappy and too tall to carry its own weight in high summer. All the same, I foresee that my border will soon become a border of flowering shrubs and the shrubby types of rose, with a solitary delphinium, over-looked in the background, to remind me of what the unlamented herbaceous border once was.

July 15, 1951

The other day I encountered a gentleman wearing amber-coloured spectacles. He was kind enough to say that I had a well-chosen range of colour in my garden. I ex-pressed some surprise at this, since it was obvious that he could not be seeing any colours in their true colour, but must be seeing them in some fantastic alteration of tincture. Yes, he said, of course I do; it amuses me; try my glasses on, he said; look at your roses; look also at your brown-tiled roofs; look at the clouds in the sky. Look, he said, handing them to me. I looked, and was instantly transferred into a different world. A volcanic eruption, or possibly an earthquake, seemed imminent. Alarming, perhaps, but how strange, how magical.

Everything had become intensified. All the greens of turf or trees had deepened. All the blues were cut out, or turned to a blackish-brown. The whites turned to a rich buttercup yellow. The most extraordinary effect of all was when you switched over to the pink variations of colour. There has been some correspondence in the Press recently about that old favourite rose, *Zéphyrine Drouhin*. Dear though she was to me, perfect in scent, vigorous in growth, magnificent in *floraison* (a lovely and expressive word we might well import from French into English, since we seem to have no equivalent in our language), and so kindly and obliging in having no thorns, never a cross word or a scratch as one picked her—dear though she was, I say, I had always deplored the crude pink of her complexion. It was her only fault. Seen through the magic glasses, she turned into a copper-orange; burnished; incredible.

Zéphyrine Drouhin has a romantic history, worthy of her breeze-like name. She derives from a hybrid found growing in 1817 in a hedge of roses in the Ile de Bourbon, now called Réunion, off the east coast of Africa. This hybrid became the parent of the whole race of Bourbon roses, which in their turn have given rise to the modern roses we call Hybrid Perpetuals and Hybrid Teas. This is putting it very briefly, and seems to bear no relation to the great pink bush flowering in the summer garden under the name *Zéphyrine Drouhin*. Who was Zéphyrine? Who was Monsieur Drouhin? These are questions I cannot answer. They sound like characters in a novel by Flaubert. I know only that this gentle, thornless, full-bosomed, generous

trollop of a rose turned into a fabulous flaming bush under
the sorcery of the tinted glasses.

July 22, 1951

Visitors to June and July flower-shows may have been
surprised, pleased, and puzzled by enormous spikes, six to
eight feet in height, which looked something like a giant
lupin, but which, on closer inspection, proved to be very
different. They were to be seen in various colours: pale
yellow, buttercup-yellow, greenish-yellow, white and
greenish-white, pink, and a curious fawn-pink which is as
hard to describe, because as subtle, as the colour of a
chaffinch's breast.

These were *Eremuri*, sometimes called the fox-tail lily
and sometimes the giant asphodel. They belong, in fact,
to the botanical family of the lilies, but, unlike most lilies,
they do not grow from a bulb. They grow from a star-
fish-like root, which is brittle and needs very careful
handling when you transplant it. I think this is probably
the reason why some people fail to establish the eremurus
satisfactorily. It should be moved in the last weeks of
September or the first weeks of October, and it should be
moved with the least possible delay. The roots should never
be allowed to wait, shrivelling, out of the ground. Plant
them instantly, as soon as they arrive from the nursery.
Spread out the roots, flat, in a rather rich loamy soil, and
cover them over with some bracken to protect them from
frost during their first winter. Plant them under the
shelter of a hedge, if you can; they dislike a strong wind,
and the magnificence of their spires will show up better
for the backing of a dark hedge. They like lime and sunshine.

Thus established, the fox-tail lily should give increasing
delight as the years go by. They get better and better as
they grow older and older, throwing up more and more

spires of flower from each crown of their star-fish root. I must admit that they cost about 7s. 6d. each, but it is a good investment. There are several sorts obtainable: the giant *Eremurus robustus*, which flowers in June, and then the smaller ones, the Shelford hybrids and the Warei hybrids in their strange colours. Splendid things; torches of pale colour, towering, dwarfing the ordinary little annuals. Aristocrats of the garden, they are well worth the three half-crowns they cost.

July 29, 1951

July is the best month for dividing the coloured primroses and polyantha, but the first week of August is not too late, especially if the ground is moist. I suppose they are amongst the easiest plants to grow; one sees them everywhere, in sun, in shade, in borders, in odd corners, most accommodating and obliging, though they do best with a little shade either from light woodland or under a north wall. They seem to prefer a rather heavy soil; and every three years or so they should be increased by division, pulling the clump gently apart and replanting the rooted pieces, a very economical method of multiplying the supply.

All this is A B C to every gardener, and it is really of the more difficult sorts that I want to write. How many of us have been tempted by the old varieties, and how many of us have come to grief! One does see the old double purple, and double lilac, and the double white which is like a tiny centifolia rose; but how seldom one sees the dark red Madame Pompadour or the Cloth of Gold. The old doubles are probably the easiest to keep going, a supposition confirmed by the fact that they are also the cheapest to buy. Jack-in-the-green, with his ruff, is reliable, but as for some of the others it must be admitted that they defy even the expert. I have been making inquiries from various growers, and find a remarkable unanimity of opinion. It seems to be generally agreed that they are gross feeders, needing a strong diet of rotted manure or compost at their roots, and a yearly change of situation because they so quickly exhaust the soil. You must either dig them up and remake their bed and replant them in it, or dig them up and replant them in a freshly prepared bed somewhere else. Feed, feed, feed, is their motto. Never allow them to become parched, and never allow the clumps to become overcrowded. The soil should be stiff, not light. Then you may hope for some success.

There are some newer varieties which have much of the charm of old primroses. *Garriard Guinevere*, with bronze leaves and pinkish-lilac flowers, is easy; so are *Betty Green*, red, and *Craddock's White*. *Marie Crousse*, pink edged with white, is not too difficult, nor are *E. R. Janes* and *Arthur Dumoulin*, which might easily be mistaken for a Parma violet. They are all worth trying, especially if you live in Scotland or Eire, where they seem best to thrive. There is something in that damp climate which suits them. If you live in England, you must try to make up to them in other ways for the softness and humidity they pine for, and lack. Homesickness overtakes them; they peter out; they die.

July 6, 1952

Most people are already familiar with the miniature roses *Roulettii* and *Oakington Ruby*, but perhaps not everyone realizes that these pretty dwarfs are now obtainable in other varieties. Seldom growing more than eight to twelve inches high, thus taking up the minimum of space, they are ideal for the very small garden, or for a child's garden, or for a rockery, or for a deep stone trough raised to eye-level where their midget blooms can be easily appreciated. I can also imagine them giving much interest and pleasure grown in the window-box of an invalid's room.

G

They are not particular as to soil, though like all roses they enjoy full sun. They can all be obtained in pots and thus can be put out at any season of the year, even now at the height of summer. They are not impossibly expensive, averaging 10s. for three, or in collections of three, five and six, ranging respectively from 10s. to 17s. 6d. Nothing extra for postage or packing.*

Some of their names are rather coy, but perhaps that was only to be expected. *Sweet Fairy*, pale pink; *Little Princess*, double white; *Baby Crimson*; *Bo Peep*, a tiny polyantha, double rose-pink; *Maïd Marion*, dark red; *Pam*, rose-pink; *Cinderella*, white flushed pink, a little more expensive at 12s. 6d. for three, the same price as *Red Elf*. Pumilla is the giant of the group, attaining fifteen inches, crimson with a white eye. *Roulettii* is still the smallest, seldom exceeding six inches.

I don't as a rule care much for roses grown as standards; they look top-heavy with their great blooms on one thin leg like a crane; but it would be a sour heart that could resist the appeal of standards nine to twelve inches in height, with flowers to scale. One of the charms, to me, of the little roses is that they give no suggestion of a cramped deformity, such as one finds in dwarfed Japanese trees. They are just simply roses seen through the wrong end of opera-glasses.

The standards, by the way, are more expensive than the bushes; they cost 10s. each.

July 13, 1952
The bushes of Mezereon or *Daphne mezereum* should now be hung with their fruits, if the birds have not already pecked them off. It is well worth while to save and sow some of them, for they germinate very freely and a crop

* From Thomas Robinson, Porchester Nurseries, Carlton, Nottingham.

of young plants is the result. I am told on good authority that the Daphne is not very long-lived but has a better expectation of life when it is growing on its own roots, i.e. has not been grafted, so the moral of growing it from seed (or cuttings) is obvious.

The Mezereon seems to share with the Madonna lily a predilection for cottage gardens. Bushes five feet high and four feet wide carry their wine-coloured bloom on the naked stems year after year in February and March in a luxuriance unknown to grander gardens where far more trouble is taken about them. Cottagers apparently just stick it in everywhere, when, with the perversity of an inverted snobbishness, it grows. It is useless to try to explain this peculiar psychology of certain plants. One must accept it and do the best one can to reproduce the conditions they appear to enjoy.

After struggling for years to induce *Daphne mezereum* to thrive in my garden, I have at last achieved a miserable degree of success by planting it in a mixture of leaf-mould and sand, in the broken shade of some trees of Kentish cob-nuts. This is the treatment I would recommend: a spongy soil with overhead shade in summer. After all, the Mezereon is sometimes claimed as a native of Britain, growing in woods, so it seems reasonable to plant it in the sort of soil it would be likely to encounter in its natural habitat, full of decayed leaves and humus, rich with the fallen wealth of centuries.

On the other hand, some people will tell you that it never thrives better than in a hot, dry place, such as a gravelly path right up against the house. So what is one to believe?

There are two kinds of *Daphne mezereum*. One is the familiar claret-coloured one, pink as a *Vin Rosé* held up to the light in a *carafe*. The other is white, *Daphne mezereum alba*. They have different-coloureb berries. The familiar one has bright red berries. The white form has bright yellow berries. I would strongly advise you to poke some seeds of both into small pots, instead of letting the birds have them. Daphnes do not transplant well, and should always be tipped straight out of a pot, like a broom or a clematis.

I have not observed seed on any of the other Daphnes, with the exception of the scentless *D. acutiloba*, but there is a prostrate one called *Blagayana*, ivory in colour and intensely sweet-scented in the early spring. This likes to be layered and weighted down with stones at every point where the layer has been inserted. It will then spread outwards into a mat of fresh growth, which may eventually attain a width of six feet or more. It is a delight to pick in the cold days of March, to bring into the warmth of a room when the honeyed smell floats round into stray corners with a suggestion of bees and summer airs. The same is true of *Daphne odora*, but that unfortunately is not quite hardy and needs the protection of glass throughout the frosty months, either in a greenhouse or under a cloche.

July 20, 1952

This week I should like to write on a subject of general gardening interest, as a change from merely recommending certain plants to grow. These remarks will inevitably apply to the larger type of garden where plants can be grown in generous masses, but I think and hope that they may also be applicable to the small garden as a matter of principle.

You see, I believe that one ought always to regard a garden in terms of architecture as well as of colour. One has huge lumps of, let us say, the shrub roses making large voluminous bushes like a Victorian crinoline, or flinging themselves about in wild sprays; or, putting it another way, some plants make round fat bushes, and seem to demand a contrast in a tall sharp plant, say delphiniums, sticking up in a cathedral spire of bright blue amongst the roses instead of in the orthodox way at the back of a herbaceous border. It is all a question of shape. Architectural shape, demanding the pointed thin ones amongst the fat rounds, as a minaret rises above the dome of a mosque.

Let me say here, for the small garden, that one might happily cause some spikes of the pink *Linaria Canon J. Went* to rise above a carpeting of low pansies or violas. This Linaria comes true from seed; sows itself everywhere like a welcome, not an unwelcome, weed; and is as pretty a thing as you could wish to have in quantities for picking for the house indoors.

Another fine thing to make great steeples is *Yucca gloriosa*. This will tower in a vast heavy ivory pyramid in July, of a powerful architectural value. It does not flower every year, so you must have at least three plants in order to get a yearly blooming, and for this you need a certain amount of space. I did begin by saying that this article would be addressed to people with the larger type of garden; but if the smaller garden can spare even three yards of room in a corner, *Yucca gloriosa* will come as a fine surprise on the grand scale in July, and will carry out my contention that you want variety of shape and height to make an aesthetic composition instead of just an amorphous muddle. The Yucca, being a child of the desert in Mexico and some of the hotter parts of the United States, such as California, likes the driest possible place and the sunniest, but on the whole accommodates itself very obligingly to our soil and climate.

July 27, 1952

Often I am asked to recommend hedging plants for small or brand-new gardens, sometimes in order to shut out the neighbour, sometimes in order to shut out livestock of any size from rabbits to cows. Usually, for the former, I fall back upon hornbeam, which is rapid of growth, inexpensive to buy, pleasant to look at, whether green in spring and summer or brown in autumn or winter, a grand nesting place for birds, and willing to grow to any height you want it, up to fifteen or twenty feet if necessary. For the latter, I think at once of those two great stand-bys, *Berberis Darwinii* and *Berberis stenophylla*, so decorative in the early part of the year with their orange and yellow flowers, respectively; both evergreen, with dark blue berries in autumn. Rabbits are said to have a particular but understandable aversion to making their way through a hedge of prickly berberis.

I now realize, however, that there are a lot of hedging plants which I have never hitherto recommended in this column. *Pyracantha*, for example. We are all well accustomed to seeing *Pyracantha* growing up the wall of a house, smothered in red or yellow berries in autumn, but it is seldom recognized that it will make a fine thorny hedge, obedient to any amount of clipping, and angry enough with its thorns to keep out any invader. I would recommend *Pyracantha Lalandii* or *Pyracantha augustifolia* to make a tough hedge, disagreeable to intruders but agreeable to yourselves, looking out on to it from the windows of your house.

There are many other things that may be planted to form a break between your garden and the next. A hedge of lilac, for instance; or a hedge of *Cydonia*, the Japanese quince, which most people still call Japonica, now called *Chaenomeles*; or a hedge of the shrubby roses which need so little attention; or a hedge of *Osmanthus Delavayii*, evergreen, with sweet-scented white flowers in April or May. There are endless variations possible. No need to stick to the old privet or laurel of our Victorian grandfathers, dark, dank, dusty, and dull—how deadly dull.

August

August 5, 1951

IN the summer days before the war, the village flower-show, which would be better called a produce-show, was quite a grand affair. There were two marquees, large enough to dwarf the Miniature-Gardens-on-Plates and the Victorian-Posy-in-an-Egg-cup into looking even tinier. The Supper-dish for Five People at one and nine-pence did not necessarily have to be meatless in 1939. The local nurserymen staged handsome exhibits *Not for competition*, raising the standard and causing the Amateurs-without-help (Class A), the Amateurs-with-help (Class B), and the cottagers (Class C), Each Entry 2d., to exclaim 'Coo, look at that!' determined that next year at the show they would try to emulate their professional neighbours.

Those good days disappeared for a time; the village could no longer afford marquees, and had to arrange its show, more modestly, in any shelter it could get: the corrugated-iron shelter of the Women's Institute, or the Parish Room, or a barn borrowed from a farmer. It had to be staged somehow or somewhere, to keep the show going and to prevent interest from dying out.

Now, better days are returning. Marquees have re-appeared, and the big nurserymen of the county are again willing to show their wares. The sumptuous effect of the Best Box of Vegetables again graces the trestle tables and how magnificent they are in shape and colour, those mixed collections of red tomatoes, orange carrots, ivory parsnips, pale potatoes freshly washed in milk, jade-green lettuce, blood-red beetroot, emerald peas, with one pod split open, and marrows like stranded whales.

How fine, indeed, in their assembly are the fruits of the earth, simply, and by cottagers, displayed. Great hairy gooseberries set out on kitchen plates; black-currants the size of marbles; raspberries like pink thimbles made for a giantess; and some soft peaches and brown figs from the greenhouse of an Amateur-with-help. How rural are the eggs, the bunches of herbs, the home-made cakes, the coloured jars of jam, the golden honey. How pretty the baskets of mixed flowers, and how touching the jam-pots of wild-flowers and grasses collected by the children.

Everyone comes in clothes that seem to match the exhibits, flowered frocks, bright scarves, and here and there a sunbonnet. The children have been scrubbed until their cheeks shine. One knows that they are little scamps really, but to-day you could not convince even a policeman that they had ever climbed the gate into an orchard. There are some speeches, and everybody says something amiable about everybody else; local feuds are forgotten for the day. There is no ill-feeling when the red, blue, and green tickets meaning 1st, 2nd, and 3rd prizes have been hopefully inspected on the cards, nor any grievance against the glum silence of no ticket at all, for it is recognized that the judges have been fair and impartial. Someone is in charge of a gramophone, and in the evening after the prizes have been distributed there may be some dancing in the field outside. The corn is ripening down in the valley; the young moon hangs over the church tower, and a little breeze springs up to ruffle the leaves of the poplars.

I love the village flower-show; I prefer it even to the village fête, or *feet* as they usually pronounce it. This has a Bank Holiday tang about it, with a loud-speaker van blaring away, and squalid litter left blowing about somebody's garden. What I like about the show is its complete lack of self-consciousness. Here is no organized entertainment: no folk-dancing at 5 p.m. which might once have been spontaneous but now certainly isn't, except in a few remote villages; no one selling raffle tickets for a bottle of whisky; no pot-shots taken with darts at the effigy of some unpopular foreign dictator. The village show is honest-to-God, whatever that may mean, and I think it does mean something. It means honest work and long experience, no nonsense about green fingers, which is one of the most slip-shod, easy-going, indulgent expressions ever invented. Ask any gardener or countryman what he thinks of it, and you will be rewarded as you deserve by a slow cynical grin and no verbal answer at all, except possibly 'Green fingers, my foot!'

He knows better. He knows that hard digging, rich feeding, deep knowledge, and constant care, are the only way to produce the prize-winning exhibits he puts on to the trestle tables at his annual local show, for the admiration and esteem of his neighbours in competition.

There is no short cut to success in prize-taking, or to the silver trophy which has to be won three years running for the best exhibit on points and which will eventually stand between the pair of Staffordshire china dogs on the mantelpiece in the front parlour, suitably inscribed with the name of the winner, a record of triumph, and (one hopes) an incentive to his children and grandchildren for many years to come.

August 5, 1951

A lot of people have a lot of trouble with lilies. I have myself. I try. I fail. I despair. Then I try again. Only last week did it occur to me to go and ask for advice from a famous grower of lilies in my neighbourhood, which was the obvious and sensible thing to do. I might have thought of it before. Surely he will not mind my passing on the hints he gave me, especially if it leads to an encouragement to grow some varieties of this supremely beautiful family.

There are four cardinal points, he said, like the compass. Point 1: good drainage is essential; no stagnant moisture, even if it means digging out a hole and putting a layer of crocks or coarse clinker at the bottom. Point 2: make up a suitable bed to receive your bulbs, a bed rich in humus, which means leaf-mould, peat, compost, chopped bracken, or whatever form of humus you can command. Point 3: never plant lily bulbs which have been out of the ground too long or have had their basal roots cut off. Reject these, even if you find them offered at cheap rates in the horticultural department of some chain stores. Lily bulbs should be lifted fresh and replanted quickly, with their basal roots intact; therefore it is advisable to obtain them from any reputable nurseryman, who will pack them in moist peat and will never allow them to dry out before despatch. Point 4: divide when they become overcrowded.

To these hints I might add another. Most lilies dislike what professional gardeners call 'movement of air,' which in plain English means wind or a draught. I have also discovered by experience that the Regal lily, *L. regale*, likes growing amongst some covering shelter such as Southernwood (Old Man) or one of the artemisias, I suppose because the foliage gives protection to the young lily-growth against late frosts, but also because some plants take kindly to one another in association. Certainly the long white trumpets of the lily look their majestic best emerging above the grey-green cloud of these fluffy, gentle, aromatic herbs.

These notes on lilies are absurdly incomplete. I thought I would amplify them next Sunday, especially because August is the month to plant the Madonna lily, the *Lilium candidum*, that virginal lily, the flower of the Annunciation,

which flourishes for the cottager and often refuses to flourish
in grander gardens.

August 12, 1951

Promises must be fulfilled. I said I would write something more about lilies, especially the Madonna lily, *Lilium
candidum*, whose bulbs ought to be planted in this month
of August. Never having grown it successfully, I am the
last person to preach about it, and my remarks must be
taken as theoretical.

> Where did Gabriel get a lily
> In the month of March?

I once read, and have never forgotten, those two lines
in a poem I have never been able to trace. * Wherever that

---

* It so happened that the author of these lines read this article and
sent me the full text of the poem, which had been 'written many
years ago and appeared in *Country Life*.' She has now given me
permission to reprint it here.

LADY DAY

> Where did Gabriel get a lily,
> In the month of March,
> When the green
> Is hardly seen
> On the early larch?
>   Though I know
>   Just where they grow,
> I have pulled no daffodilly.
> Where did Gabriel get a lily
> In the month of March?
>   Could I bring
>   The tardy Spring
>   Under Her foot's arch,
>   Near or far
>   The primrose star
> Should bloom with violets,—willy-nilly.
>   Where did Gabriel get a lily
>   In the month of March?
>   GRACE JAMES

bright Archangel found his lily, it was certainly not in the more ambitious sort of garden. It prefers the humbler home. There is an old tradition that the Madonna lily throve best in cottage gardens because the housewife was in the habit of chucking out her pail of soap-suds all over the flower-bed. Curiously enough, this tradition is now confirmed by the advice that the young growth of these lilies should be sprayed with a lather of soft-soap and water, to prevent the disease called botrytis. Thus do these old-wives' tales sometimes justify themselves.

The Madonna lily should be planted now without delay. There is a variety called *Salonica*, because it grows there, which is said to be more resistant to botrytis, but whichever variety you plant put in the bulbs so shallow as to rest almost on top of the soil, showing their noses. If you bury them too deep they will have to shove themselves up in that wise way that plants have, knowing what suits them even better than we know, but this is giving them a lot of trouble and struggle which you might have spared them. So plant them shallow, and plant them as soon as they arrive; don't leave the bulbs lying about to get dry. And once planted, leave them alone. Don't dig them up to move them to another place. Let them stay put. They are not modern-minded, wanting to roam about; they are statically minded; they are fond of their home, once you have induced them to take to it.

The Madonna lily is an exception to the general rule that lilies demand plenty of humus. It likes lime, which may take the form of old mortar rubble, and it likes a scratchy soil. The scratchy soil idea confirms the old theory that part of their success in cottage gardens was due to the fact that the grit from the surface of the lanes blew over the hedge and worked its way into the ground. Even to-day, when few country lanes are tarred, this may still hold good, and I have known cottagers send out their little boys with a shovel and a box mounted on old pram wheels to collect grit for the garden. It is never wise to disregard the sagacity of those who do not learn their lore from books.

August 19, 1951

People often ask what plants are suitable for a shady situation, by which they mean either the north side of a wall or house, or in the shadow cast by trees. There are so many such plants that no one need despair. A number of shrubby things will do well, such as the azaleas, the Kalmias, the rhododendrons, and a pretty, seldom seen, low-growing shrub with waxy white pendent flowers called *Zenobia pulverulenta*, always provided that the soil is lime-free for all these subjects. The many cotoneasters and berberis have no objection to shade, and are less pernickety as to soil. *Daphne laureola* will thrive, and so will *Viburnum Burkwoodii*, very easy and sweet-scented, making a big bush. The well-known Snowberry, *Symphoricarpus racemosus*, will grow anywhere and is attractive in autumn with its ivory berries and tangle of black twigs. And if you want something more choice than the Snowberry, there are many magnolias which enjoy the protection of a north wall: *M. Lennei*, wine-pink; *M. Soulangeana*, white; and *M. liliflora nigra*, a deep claret colour, which has the advantage of a very long-flowering season, all through May and June, with a few odd flowers appearing even in July and August. The magnolias all appreciate some peat or leaf-mould to fill in the hole you dig out when you plant them, and it is important not to let them suffer from drought before they have had time to become established.

If, however, you have no space for these rather large shrubs, there are plenty of things other than shrubs to fill up an un-sunny border. There are the foxgloves, which can now be obtained in varieties far superior to the woodland foxglove, flowering all round the stem, and in colours

preferable to the old magenta, lovely though that may look
in the woods. The Excelsior strain flowers all round; you
can get seed from Messrs. Sutton, Reading. The columbines
will also tolerate shade, and there is a blue one called
Hensol Harebell which I think looks better in an out-of-
the-way corner than the long-spurred garden varieties.
There is also a charming old plant called *Astrantia*, the
Masterwort, seldom seen now except in cottage gardens,
which will ramp away in an unpromising shady place
and increase itself by seed. The *Epimediums* should not
be overlooked; they make clumps of pretty foliage and
throw up delicate sprays of flower like tiny orchids in
May. The hellebores and the lily-of-the-valley, the primroses and the polyanthus, the candelabra primulas, and,
as you grow more ambitious, the blue poppy *Meconopsis
Baileyii*, which is the dream of every gardener, will all
take happily to a shaded home, especially if some moisture
keeps them fresh.

August 26, 1951

In the hope of picking up some new ideas, I have just
spent ten days visiting gardens, either famous or modest,
in the West of England. My interest was concentrated on
the shrubs or trees or climbers that one might find flowering
at this jejune time of year; something I didn't know, or
else through ignorance or prejudice had never attempted
to grow. I must say at once that I was converted to some
of the hydrangeas, not the mop-headed sort called *hortensis*,
but the sort with a flat centre ringed with open flowers.
They are known as *Hydrangea aspera*, and there are some
decorative forms called *villosa* and *Sargentiana*. A well-
grown bush, pouring over a paved path or covering the
angle of a flight of steps, is a rich and rewarding sight
in August, when everything becomes heavy and dark and
lumpish.

I was also impressed by the sight of acanthus in flower. Not only has this plant very noble leaves, looking fine and classical at any time of year, but its mauve flower spike is of great value in the August border. I saw also an immense growth of *Cotoneaster rotundifolia*, sweeping its petticoats to the ground, as in an old-time curtsey, red-berried among its small, dark green leaves. I saw also a little tree which particularly took my fancy; this was the Bladder Senna, *Colutea arborescens*, with bronze, pea-like flowers and large seed-pods looking as though they would pop with a small bang, like a blown-up paper bag, if you burst them between your hands. This little tree amused me, because it carried its flowers and its seed-pods at the same time. In one garden where I saw it the pods were turning pink, very pretty amongst the bronzy flowers.

The indigoferas were much in evidence, making me wonder, as I had often wondered before, why these graceful shrubs were not more freely planted. They throw out long sprays, seven or eight feet in length, dangling with pinkish, vetch-like flowers in August and September. *Indigofera Potanini* is a pale, pretty pink; *I. Gerardiana* is deeper in colour, with more mauve in it, and is perhaps the more showy of the two. They should both, I think, be planted in conjunction, so that their sprays can mingle in a cloud of the two different colours. I should like to see them combined with a front planting of a lovely new scabious, called *Grey Lady*, which I also discovered on my travels, and backed by a grey-blue clematis called *Perle d'azur*. Anyone fortunate enough to have a wall could train the clematis on that, otherwise a couple of tall poles would support it.

August 3, 1952

This is the moment to order and plant the bulbs of *Amaryllis Belladonna*, commonly called the Belladonna lily. Unlike Milton's Amaryllis, she will not sport in the shade; in fact she demands the hottest and sunniest place to produce her flowers at all. Given such a place, however, at the foot of a south-facing wall, or, ideally, a greenhouse wall, she will produce sheaves of pinkish-mauve trumpets on a naked stem which is in itself of a beautiful bloomy plum colour, in late September and October, just at the time when flowers for the house are rare, apart from the dahlias and chrysanthemums and the Japanese anemone.

Amaryllis Belladonna, who is threatened before long with a change of name to *Callicore rosea*, is a native of South Africa and is reasonably hardy in the southern half of England. I would not recommend her for northern gardens, unless she could command special care, by which I mean protection in winter and at that ticklish moment when the growth begins to appear above the ground. In spring, the bulbs throw up their leaf growth, and should then be kept well watered while the leaves are green. A mulch of rotted manure or compost or leaf-mould will help, spread over the ground in May. When the leaves turn yellow and die down the bulbs can be left to themselves, to get dry and sun-baked, waiting for the flower to appear in autumn. They cost about 2s. each; or for anyone who can afford to be more extravagant, the variety called *rubra* can be obtained at 5s. a bulb, and will throw a flower of a deeper, richer pink. This all sounds extravagant, but you will be surprised to find how quickly the bulbs increase in quantity after a few years, when they can be lifted in July or August, and the new little bulbs replanted to extend the clump. They can be expected to come to flowering size within a year or two. You can, if you like, regard this as a hint to cadge within the next few weeks some thinnings of overcrowded bulbs from the garden of a fortunate friend. But do remember that sun is all-important. It is remarkable what a difference even

Sir Walter Scott   Princess Victoria.

Miss Miller.   Emperor of China

a few hours of afternoon shade will make to the crop of
flowers. I know, because I have tried it, some in sun all
day, and some in partial shade. The ones in partial shade
don't flower at all; the ones in full sun flower generously.

August 10, 1952

I have a myrtle growing on a wall. It is only the
common myrtle, *Myrtus communis*, but I think you would
have to travel far afield to find a lovelier shrub for July
and August flowering. The small, pointed, dark-green
leaves are smothered at this time of year by a mass of
white flowers with quivering centres of the palest green-
yellow, so delicate in their white and gold that it appears as
though a cloud of butterflies had alighted on the dark shrub.

The myrtle is a plant full of romantic associations in
mythology and poetry, the sacred emblem of Venus and
of love, though why Milton called it brown I never could
understand, unless he was referring to the fact that the
leaves, which are by way of being evergreen, do turn
brown in frosty weather or under a cold wind. Even if it
gets cut down in winter there is nothing to worry about,
for it springs up again, at any rate in the South of England.
In the north it might be grateful for a covering of ashes
or fir branches over the roots. It strikes very easily from
cuttings, and a plant in a pot is a pretty thing to possess,
especially if it can be stood near the house-door, where the
aromatic leaves may be pinched as you go in and out. In
very mild counties, such as Cornwall, it should not require
the protection of a wall, but may be grown as a bush or
small tree in the open, or even, which I think should be
most charming of all, into a small grove suggestive of
Greece and her nymphs.

The flowers are followed by little inky berries, which
in their turn are quite decorative, and would probably
grow if you sowed a handful of them.

H

In this connection, I might mention the Bog myrtle, though it is not really a myrtle except in common parlance. It is a native of Britain, and thus by some people might be regarded as a weed, but for its strong, resinous scent, which gives it its second lovely name, Sweet Gale; it is well worth bringing in from the moors if you come across it, and give it a place in a rough corner, where it will catch the prevailing wind. It does, however, exact a purely acid soil, as peaty as possible, so is of no use to the dwellers on chalk or lime. The more moisture it gets the better, when it will spread by means of its underground roots. Travellers across Dartmoor may remember getting unexpected whiffs, like passing through a pine forest on a warm day.

August 17, 1952

The bulb catalogues arrive by every post, leaving us in a state of confused temptation. It is suitable to remember that to-day, August 17th, is the feast of Saint Hyacinth, who lived in Poland during the thirteenth century, though Saint Hyacinth has nothing to do with the bulbs we are about to order for planting in fibre in bowls or outdoors in the garden. It would be far more appropriate to remember the pagan Hyacinthus, the beautiful youth beloved of Apollo, who changed the boy's murdered body into the flower we still call by his name.

In so short an article I can do no more than mention a few of the bulbs I cannot resist. This will just be a personal list representing a personal taste. Taking the tulips first, I like the great yellow *Mongolia*, and the great white *Carrara* and *Zwannenberg*. I like *The Bishop*, deep violet in colour, sturdy and reliable, on a strong stem, tall, coming up year after year. I like the little fringed-edged *Sundew*, of a deep rose colour, cheap at 5s. a dozen and seldom seen. I like all the fantastic Parrot tulips, wild in their colouring, floppy in their growth, not stiff as the Darwins, a tulip to pick for the house rather than to regard as a flower for the garden. Then I like the broken tulips, the Rembrandts, Bizarres, and the Bybloemens, all in their different feathery stripes and flakes; and I must not omit the early little *Couleur Cardinal*, which puts up as pretty and neat a chalice of plummy bloom as any ecclesiastic could wish to see. I always think of it as a young nephew of *The Bishop*, and should like to see them planted together. Nepotism, if you like to call it that. Only they would not flower at the same time.

Leaving the tulips, we come to the narcissi; and here again we find ourselves in a confusion. I cannot here cope with the innumerable sorts, but would like to draw your attention to some of the smaller ones, *Canaliculatus*, for instance, so sweet-scented, and *Triandrus albus*, called Angel's Tears; and also to the single jonquil, bright yellow and strong of scent. These are treasures for the appreciative grower.

Please do not forget the fritillaries. They cost so little, 3s. a dozen, and they increase so surprisingly in grass. They sow themselves, appearing in odd corners where they were never planted.

August 24, 1952

I know I have written before now about the advantages of raising lilies from seed, but that was several years ago, and I think I might return to the charge. This method of obtaining lilies for nothing requires a considerable amount of patience, three to four years before you get a bulb old enough to flower, but how rewarding is the result. It also ensures that your bulbs have not been left lying about to dry up, a fatal destiny for any lily. It means also that you are not getting a stock infected by any virus disease; the plants may develop it later on, since no one can guarantee against this, but at least you know that you have started clean.

I have found that seeds sown in fairly deep pans will make little bulbs ready to plant out in their second season. The seeds can also be sown in a prepared seed-bed in drills in the open, but pans are more easily controlled, especially in the matter of weeding. Stand them on a floor of ashes to prevent the incursion of undesirable insects.

Lilies, in my experience, are tricky and unpredictable. Some of them do not object to lime in the soil; others will have nothing to say to it. For this division of taste you must consult the catalogue of a good lily nurseryman,* which will give you detailed comments on each separate variety. I cannot generalize here; but as I recently had the benefit of a visit from a well-known lily grower, I might pass on some crumbs of his wisdom.

Good drainage, he said, is essential to all lilies; they like moisture, but they will not tolerate a wetly stagnant bed. Therefore, when you dig out the site in which you intend to plant them, filling it up with the kind of soil they require—leaf mould and loam and sand as a general rule—make sure it has a layer of rough drainage placed at the bottom. Then, he said, lilies dislike being blown about by the wind, so give them an abode within the shelter of shrubs. Finally, he said, remember that nothing makes a finer mulch than bracken cut green, chopped up into short pieces, and allowed to rot. He deprecated the use of lawn-grass mowings; of artificial fertilizers; and of over-fresh organic manure. Manure, he said, should never be allowed to come into contact with the bulb itself: it should be placed well beneath it, or used as a top mulch. Bone meal, he said, was always safe and useful.

* For instance, Messrs. Constable or Messrs. Wallace, see p. 175 for addresses.

August 31, 1952

A note on some roses not often seen. *Comtesse du Cayla,* *
a China rose, so red in the stem on young wood as to appear
transparent in a bright light; very pointed in the coral-
coloured bud; very early to flower, continuing to flower
throughout the summer until the frosts come (I once picked
a bunch on Christmas morning); somewhat romantic in
her associations, for the lady in whose honour she is named
was the mistress of Louis XVIII; altogether a desirable rose,
not liable to black spot or mildew; needing little pruning
apart from the removal of wood when it has become too
old, say, every two or three years. *Mutabilis,* or *Rosa
Turkestanica,* * makes an amusing bush, five to six feet high
and correspondingly wide, covered throughout the summer
with single flowers in different colours, yellow, dusky red,
and coppery, all out at the same time. It is perhaps a trifle
tender, and thus a sheltered corner will suit this particular
harlequin.

If you want a very vigorous climber, making an incredible
length of growth in one season, do try to obtain *Rosa filipes.* *
It is ideal for growing into an old tree, which it will quickly
drape with pale-green dangling trails and clusters of small
white yellow-centred flowers. I can only describe the
general effect as lacy, with myriads of little golden eyes
looking down at you from amongst the lace. This sounds
like a fanciful description, of the kind I abhor in other
writers on horticultural subjects, but really there are times
when one is reduced to such low depths in the struggle
to convey the impression one has oneself derived, on some
perfect summer evening when everything is breathless,
and one just sits, and gazes, and tries to sum up what one
is seeing, mixed in with the sounds of a summer night—

* *Comtesse du Cayla* and *R. Turkestanica* from Messrs. T. Hilling;
address on p. 177. *Rosa filipes* from J. Russell, Sunningdale Nurseries,
Windlesham, Surrey.

the young owls hissing in their nest over the cowshed, the bray of a donkey, the plop of an acorn into the pool.

Filipes means thread-like, or with thread-like stems, so perhaps my comparison to lace is not so fanciful, after all. Certainly the reticulation of the long strands overhead, clumped with the white clusters, faintly sweet-scented, always makes me think of some frock of faded green, trimmed with Point d'Alençon—or is it Point de Venise that I mean?

September

September 2, 1951

IT surprises me always when people fail to recognize the common rosemary. 'What is that?' they say, looking at the great dark-green bushes that sprawl so generously over the paths at the entrance to the place where I live. I should have thought that rosemary was one of our most common plants, if only for the sake of its sentimental associations. It was said to have the peculiar property of strengthening the memory, and thus became a symbol of fidelity for lovers. 'A sprig of it hath a dumb language,' said Sir Thomas More; and another legend connects it with the age of Our Lord, thirty-three years, after which it stops growing in height but never in width. A romantic plant, yet so oddly, it seems, unknown.

There are several different forms of the rosemary. There is the ordinary bushy type, *Rosemarinus officinalis*, which can be grown either as a bush or clipped into shape as a hedge. I don't like it so well as a hedge, because the constant clipping means the loss of the flowers which are half its beauty, but all the same it makes a dense neat hedge if you want one. Do not cut back into the old wood. Then there is the Corsican rosemary, *R. angustifolius Corsicus* with a more feathery growth of leaf and bright blue flowers, almost gentian blue; it is less tough-looking than the common rosemary, and perhaps not quite so hardy, but so lovely a thing that it well deserves a sheltered corner. It hates cold winds. The fastigiate or pyramidal rosemary, pleasingly called *Miss Jessup's Upright*, will make sentinels six feet high within a couple of years. (Who was Miss Jessup, I wonder?) There is also a creeping form, suitable for rock-gardens, called *prostratus*, but this is not very hardy and I would not recommend it to anybody not living in the warmer counties. If it can be persuaded to thrive, however, as it might be induced to do with its roots sheltering a long way back between stones, away from frost and damp, it makes a grateful mat of evergreen and a good covering plant for little early bulbs coming up through it, such as the Lady Tulip, *T. Clusiana*, or the jonquils, or the miniature narcissi such as *N. juncifolius*, so sweet scented.

It should not be forgotten, either, that a white-flowered form of the common rosemary is obtainable, making a change from the blue-flowered form more usually seen.

Most of the rosemaries will flourish anywhere in the sun, preferring a light soil, even a poor sandy stony soil, and will root very easily from cuttings taken off in September, stuck firmly into sand, and left to grow on until next spring when they can be planted out.

September 9, 1951

A most pleasing and original suggestion reaches me in a nurseryman's catalogue. It is the sort of suggestion which could provide extra colour and interest in a small garden, without taking up too much space and without involving too much labour. It is, simply, the idea of growing low Alpines in a narrow border on both sides of the path running from your gate to your door, or, of course, on both sides or even one side of any path you may find suitable.

By 'low' Alpines I do not mean those plants which occur only on the lower slopes of mountains, a technical term in horticulture, as opposed to the 'high' Alpines. I mean flat-growing; close to the ground; the sorts that make little tufts and squabs and cushions and pools of colour when in

flower, and neat tight bumps of grey or green for the rest
of the year when the flowers have gone over. The range
of choice is wide. Saxifrages, silene, stonecrops, thrift,
Raoulia, acaene, androsace, aubrietia in moderation, thyme,
Achillea argentea, *Erinus alpinis*, *Tunica saxifraga*, *Morisia
hypogea*, *Bellis Dresden China*, sempervivum or houseleeks,
some campanulas such as *C. garganica*, so easy and self-
sowing—the list is endless, and gives scope for much
variety.

* * *

I would not restrict it only to the rugs and mats and
pillows, but would break its level with some inches of
flower-stalks, such as the orange Alpine poppy, *Papaver
alpinum*, and some violas such as *V. gracilis* or *V. Bosnaica*,
and some clumps of dianthus such as the Cheddar pink
or the prettily named Dad's Favourite, and even some
primroses specially chosen, such as *rosea* or *Garriard
Ganymede* or *Betty Green*, and any other favourite which
may occur to you. This list is not intended to dictate. It
is intended only to suggest that a ribbon or band of colour,
no more than twelve inches wide, might well wend its
flat way beside a path in even the most conventional
garden.

But if you had a garden on a slope, in a hilly district,
what an opportunity would be yours! Then your flat ribbon
would become a rill, a rivulet, a beck, a burn, a brook,
pouring crookedly downhill between stones towards the
trout-stream flowing along the valley at the bottom I
suppose some people do possess gardens like that, in
Gloucestershire for instance, or in Cumberland, or in the
Highlands. Let those fortunate ones take notice, and,
dipping an enormous paint-brush into the wealth offered
by the autumn catalogues, splash its rainbow result
wherever their steps may lead them.

September 16, 1951

A correspondent wants me to write about gadgets. He points out, with commendable good sense, that one hesitates to spend money on such things unless one can be sure that they will justify their cost. Now this is just the difficulty. I have found by experience that gadgets, however ingenious and alluring, rarely replace with advantage the old and tried tools. One always goes back, in the end, to the simple designs that have proved themselves best adapted to their use throughout the centuries. It would be hard, indeed, to improve upon the spade, the fork, the shovel, the shears, the birch-broom, the rake, or even the little humble trowel.

Nevertheless there are certain things which one discovers during a life-time of gardening, not gadgets exactly, but helpful hints. I see that I shall have to make two articles out of this subject, the first one to be concerned entirely with string. For example, I find it far more economical to buy a huge ball of hop-twine, such as we use in our Kentish hop-gardens, three times the size of any known football, instead of many balls of tarred twine. As hop-twine will last for two or three years without rotting, it is invaluable for securing big shrubs or shrub-roses to their stakes. It is also possible to buy old stock of telephone wire by the mile, the wire enclosed in some sort of rubber, at £2 15s. a mile, but who wants a mile? And anyway, I find that the rubber soon perishes. Far more generally useful are those spools of green twist, which, neatly rolled in a paper cylinder, mendaciously imply that they will remain tidily exuding their life down to its last inch. Surely I am not the only gardener to find that after the first fifty yards or so you come up against an impossible tangle, when, in desperation, you cut disorderly ends here and there.

A way out of this muddle is to put your spool into a tin, say an old slug-bait tin, piercing a hole in the top of the lid. You should pierce the hole *outwards*, otherwise the

jagged points of the hole will catch the string, interrupting
its free run.

Another brief hint. One can now buy packets of paper
strips about four inches long and a quarter of an inch wide,
reinforced by a thin wire up the middle, which makes
them both flexible and tough. You twiddle them into any
circlet you want and thus save all that business of tying
knots—usually granny knots, I suspect. They save a lot
of time, where a light, temporary tie is needed, for tall,
brittle annuals such as Salpiglossis or even sweet peas, if
you are growing them on the ambitious, single-stem
system for exhibition.

September 23, 1951

More gadgets. The essence of a gadget is that it shall
be (*a*) small and (*b*) unknown to other people. It must be
one's own discovery; something that one has found out for
oneself. The rubber-tyred wheelbarrow is thus too large
and too well known to be called a gadget; but what a weight
of wheeling, and what a sparing of turf, it saves! A little
companion I would not be without is the fern-trowel; it
is long and narrow, indispensable for weeding between
small plants, such as you might find in a rockery or a
stone-trough-garden. Like all the hand-tools, it should be
of stainless steel, bright to look at and easy to clean. (A
rag wrung out of paraffin should be mentioned here.)
Pocket-sized secateurs may meet with contempt from the
professional gardener, who is usually a scornful man, but
should be constantly carried by the amateur. Speaking for
myself, I am a miserable lost creature whenever I mislay
my Wilkinson Sword secateurs. Less portable, but still very
useful, are the soluble flower-pots obtainable in various
sizes; they are for seedlings that do not enjoy being transplanted and prefer being dropped straight into the ground in
their home-pot which will quickly dissolve in the damp earth.

Labels. I wish I had good advice to give about labels; they are always my worry. The strong metal label called Acme, which can be printed with any name or date you like, is completely satisfactory but much too expensive for anything except the permanent trees or shrubs. What I want is a nice neat label which I can write for myself, and set to mark, say, a dozen special daffodils or some chosen bulbs; but, as we all know, white paint is not what it once was, and indelible ink is now only too delible. *

This article seems to be deteriorating from a list into something more like a grumble. The time has come for me to lift it out of this rut, with a more constructive suggestion. I have one to make. It is about a belt, the sort of belt you wear round your waist. It could be made of strong buckram or of leather, and it should not be beyond the skill of any cobbler or harness-maker. From the belt would dangle every minor adjunct that the amateur gardener wandering round his garden could possibly wish to have ready to his hand: a roll of string, a knife, a tin of slug-bait, a pencil, a tin to collect seeds, a trowel, secateurs. . . . Each to his choice and need. A belt that Alice's White Knight would have approved. I might take out a patent for it.†

September 30, 1951

The more I see of other people's gardens the more convinced do I become of the value of good grouping and shapely training. These remarks must necessarily apply most forcibly to gardens of a certain size, where sufficient space is available for large clumps or for large specimens of individual plants, but even in a small garden the spotty

* Messrs. Woodman, High Street, Pinner, supply the best answer to my problem.

† May I here make a grateful acknowledgment to the kind and clever *Observer* reader who made and sent me one, exactly to this specification?

effect can be avoided by massing instead of dotting plants here and there.

It is a truly satisfactory thing to see a garden well schemed and wisely planted. Well schemed are the operative words. Every garden, large or small, ought to be planned from the outset, getting its bones, its skeleton, into the shape that it will preserve all through the year even after the flowers have faded and died away. Then, when all colour has gone, is the moment to revise, to make notes for additions, and even to take the mattock for removals. This is gardening on the large scale, not in details. There can be no rules, in so fluid and personal a pursuit, but it is safe to say that a sense of substance and solidity can be achieved only by the presence of an occasional mass breaking the more airy companies of the little flowers.

What this mass shall consist of must depend upon many things: upon the soil, the aspect, the colour of neighbouring plants, and above all upon the taste of the owner. I can imagine, for example, a border arranged entirely in purple and mauve—phlox, stocks, pansies, clematis Jackmanii trained over low hoops—all planted in bays between great promontories of the plum-coloured sumach, *Rhus cotinus foliis purpureis,* but many people, thinking this too mournful, might prefer a scheme in red and gold. It would be equally easy of accomplishment, with a planting of the feathery *Thalictrum glaucum, gallardias, Achillea eupatorium* (the flat-headed yellow yarrow), *helenium, Lychnis chalcedonica,* and a host of other ordinary, willing, herbaceous things. In this case, I suppose, the mass would have to be provided by bushes of something like the golden privet or the golden yew, both of which I detest when planted as 'specimens' on a lawn, but which in so aureate a border would come into their own.

The possibilities of variation are manifold, but on the main point one must remain adamant; the alternation between colour and solidity, decoration and architecture, frivolity and seriousness. Every good garden, large or small, must have some architectural quality about it; and, apart from the all-important question of the general lay-out, including hedges, the best way to achieve this imperative effect is by massive lumps of planting such as I have suggested.

I wish only that I could practise in my own garden the principles which I so complacently preach, week after week, in this column.

September 7, 1952

Writing this article away from home, I make a few notes of things seen in the course of a fortnight's motoring, things which were either new to me, or else forgotten until the reminder came along. I had forgotten, for instance, the summer-flowering mauve *Solanum crispum var. autumnalis*, so useful in August, a trifle tender, perhaps, wanting a warm south wall; and the white *Solanum jasminoides*, another August flowerer, a most graceful climber, also a trifle tender, but well worth trying in southern counties. I had forgotten the white—or, rather, creamy—*Buddleia Fallowiana alba*, with grey leaves, an uncommon thing and a pleasant change from the ordinary mauve. *Buddleia nivea* is even more grey-leaved and woolly, almost as woolly and felted as that old favourite cottage plant, *Stachys lanata*, commonly called Rabbit's Ears or Saviour's Flannel, or, in Scotland, Lamb's Lugs. I had forgotten *Itea illicifolia*, a wall shrub with long, grey-white catkins of soft beauty, an evergreen, fragrant and, alas, tender; and *Berberis trifoliata*, expressly made to appeal to anyone with a liking for glaucous foliage.

Then I saw also a shrubby plant which I was later enabled to identify as *Abelia grandiflora*. This struck me as a surprisingly pretty shrub; it throws a wealth of pointed, bright pink buds, opening into pink-white flowers. It is quite hardy, and I would recommend it to anyone who wants some colour in the August–September garden.

Another shrub I saw was *Descaisnea Fargesii*. This is called the bean-plant, because it develops bright-blue seed-pods in autumn; very decorative. It is quite hardy and should be planted in any unwanted corner, just for the sake of its yellow-green flowers and its steel-blue pods in autumn.

These are all just notes; but I must end by urging you to grow *Indigofera pendula*. This is a surprisingly lovely thing. It arches in long sprays of pinkish-mauve pea-like flowers, growing ten feet high, dangling very gracefully from its delicate foliage. It combines very prettily with the mauve Solanum I mentioned above; or, I can imagine, with the August-flowering blue Ceanothus, *Gloire de Versailles*, or even mingling with the blue plumbago, *Ceratostigma Willmottiana*.

If you have any difficulty in finding any of these shrubs, Messrs. Hillier have them all. Address on p. 175.

September 14, 1952

I revert to some ideas I picked up while motoring away from home. One learns a lot from seeing other people's gardens. There were some roses I saw: *Independence*, for instance, of a colour difficult to describe. The nearest I can get to it is tomato lightly brushed with grey. It might associate well with the coppery polyantha *Fashion*, a very effective rose, lacking the subtlety of *Independence*, but a fine showy thing for a bed and for picking. There is a whole range now of these coppery-orange roses, *Catalonia*, *United Nations*, and *Opera* are all good; and for a fine rich yellow, with a particularly sweet scent, *Spun Gold* should come as the discovery it was to me. It was a discovery to the present grower, who found it accidentally.* By what

* Miss Hilda Murrell, address under Edwin Murrell Ltd. on p. 177, from whom the other roses mentioned can also be obtained.

I can only imagine to be a printer's error, it is accorded only one X for scent in the catalogue; in my opinion it deserves three XXX.

There are also the bi-coloured roses, yellow on one side of the petal, red-orange on the other, making an extraordinarily brilliant effect. They resemble the old briar *Austrian Copper*, well known to rose-lovers but often their despair, owing to its tendency to black-spot and die-back; and they resemble also that blazing shrub-cum-climber, *Réveil Dijonnais*, which a gardener-acquaintance of mine firmly calls Revil Die-Johnny. This should be more often planted, for it is extremely showy and goes on flowering at intervals throughout the summer; it suffers, however, from one terrible fault: it fades into a really dreadful sickly-mauve, so if you have not the leisure to pick off the dying flowers every morning before breakfast you had better give it a miss.

If, however, you like the bi-coloured roses, as I do, and want something more reliable than *Austrian Copper* in the same colouring please consider planting *Sultane* and *Madame Dieudonné*.

I see that this article has turned itself into a symphony of all the wild sunset colours, a sort of western sky after a stormy day. The sunset colours are not always very good mixers in a garden, happily though they may consort in the heavens. In a garden they should, I think, be kept apart from the pinks, and be given, if possible, a place to themselves. I know that few gardens nowadays can afford this extravagance of separate space, but I can still imagine a hedged-off enclosure where nothing but the glow of blood-orange-and-yellow roses should have its own way.

September 21, 1952

Readers of this column may have observed that I was away from home recently, getting ideas from other people's gardens. I did pick up one very good idea for a hedge. It is the Worcesterberry. This is a cross between the black currant and the gooseberry. It has small black gooseberry-like fruits which are said to make excellent jam; and as it grows very vigorously and is exceedingly thorny, it quickly provides the densest and most repellent protection against livestock, marauding children, and even rabbits. The hedge I saw was about seven feet high, but, of course, you could clip it if you wanted it lower, not to obscure a view. You would be wise to wear a complete suit of armour and steel gauntlets whilst thus engaged.

A correspondent kindly tells me of an attractive hedge she knows, made of Forsythia. I can imagine that this would look very gay in the spring, a barrier of thick gold, rather low, clipped square on top and sides, an operation which should take place annually immediately after the flowers have faded. *Forsythia intermedia spectabilis* would be the best variety to get; portentous as this name may appear, it represents nothing more recondite than the ordinary Forsythia now to be seen in every other roadside garden. Using it as a hedging-plant would give it a twist of originality more interesting than the usual bush-form. It would have a special advantage, in so far as it may be obtained without cost if you take the trouble to insert some cuttings next month, October, in an outdoor six-inch-deep trench filled with sharp sand. Take twelve-inch-long cuttings; strip the leaves off them; then press them firmly in, with your foot or your hand; see to it that they don't get loosened by wind or frost during the winter, and then by the spring you may look forward to having a long row of rooted cuttings ready to set out wherever you want your hedge. In fact, I can see no reason why you should not start your cuttings in the first place where you intend the hedge to be. It would save a lot of transplanting, which always checks the young growth. I never believe in moving

I

plants if one can possibly help it, unless, of course, they are becoming overcrowded and demanding division or a shift.

The Worcesterberry can be obtained from Messrs. John Scott, address on p. 175. I know they disagree with me and maintain that it doesn't make a good hedge; but all I can say is that I have seen a hedge with my own eyes.

September 28, 1952

This must be a paragraph addressed to those fortunate dwellers in a kind climate: Cornwall, Devon, the west coast of Scotland, or some parts of Wales and Ireland, for the flowering tree which caught my fancy last week is marked by one of those ominous little asterisks in nurserymen's catalogues, meaning 'not quite hardy.' It is *Lagerstroemeria indica*, sometimes known as the Crape Myrtle, though there is nothing crape-like about its fluffy pink, red, or white flowers. I cannot think how it came by so dismal a name. Pride of India is a much better one. It is a gay little tree, said to attain twenty to thirty feet in height, though the specimens I saw growing by the roadside in Italy were not more than ten to twelve feet, just tall enough to enjoy comfortably with a slight raising of the eyes. I recommend it with some diffidence, since I suspect that only an exceptionally sunny summer would bring it to the perfection of its flowering in this country. It could, of course, be grown against a wall, which would give it protection and an extra allowance of sun-baking, instead of as a standard in the open ground. A loamy soil suits it, and it should be pruned during the winter.

Another thing I noted was the Mediterranean heath, *Erica mediterranea*, grown in the unusual form of a standard. This struck me as an amusing way to train a heath, into a neat tall standard instead of a straggly spreading bush. It was not in flower when I saw it, but

I could well imagine what it would look like in March and April: a fuzz of pink on the top of a straight pole. Somewhat artificial, I admit, but the Italians are an inventive people and enjoy anything in the nature of a joke. I thought that four of these standards, one at each corner of a square flower bed, might look decorative as little sentinels, not taking up much ground-space, and agreeably green all the year round, whether in flower or not; or placed at intervals to form a small avenue bordering a path. They would not grow more than four or five feet high.

Erica mediterranea, unlike most of the heaths, does not object to the presence of a little lime in the soil, though naturally its preference is for peat. People whose gardens are on that type of soil could treat the white-flowered Tree Heath, *Erica arborea*, in a similar way; this grows much taller, even to ten feet where it is happy, but unfortunately it is somewhat tender and should thus be reserved for the warmer counties.

The heaths cost from 2s. 6d. to 5s. 6d. according to size.

October

October 7, 1951

PLAINTIVE letters reach me from time to time saying that if I do not like herbaceous borders what would I put in their place? It is quite true that I have no great love for herbaceous borders or for the plants that usually fill them—coarse things with no delicacy or quality about them. I think the only justification for such borders is that they shall be perfectly planned, both in regard to colour and to grouping; perfectly staked; and perfectly weeded. How many people have the time or the labour? The alternative is a border largely composed of flowering shrubs, including the big bush roses; but for those who still desire a mixed border it is possible to design one which will (more or less) look after itself once it has become established.

It could be carried out in various colour schemes. Here is an idea for one in red and purple and pink: Polyantha roses *Dusky Maiden, Frensham, Donald Prior*; musk roses *Wilhelm, Pink Prosperity, Cornelia, Felicia, Vanity*; the common old red herbaceous peonies, with Darwin tulips planted amongst them if you like; and a front edging of the dwarf asters and daisies such as *Dresden China* and *Rob Roy*, which make big mats and go on for ever, and even violets for early flowering, and some patches of *Fragaria indica*, the ornamental strawberry with bright red fruits all through the summer. Nor would I despise a counterpane, at intervals, of *Cotoneaster horizontalis*, crawling over the ground with its herring-bone spine, its small box-like leaves of darkest green and its brilliantly red berries in autumn.

Another idea, pale and rather ghostly, a twilight-moonlight border. *Forsythia* along the back; musk roses *Danae*, *Moonlight* and *Thisbe* in the middle; evening primroses, *Oenothera biennis*, self-sowing; *Iris ochroleuca*, tall and white and yellow; creamy peonies; and a front carpet of silver-foliaged artemisias and stachys.

Of course, these are only the roughest indications, outlines to be filled in. The main thing, it seems to me, is to have a foundation of large, tough, untroublesome plants with intervening spaces for the occupation of annuals, bulbs, or anything that takes your fancy. The initial outlay would seem extravagant, but at least it would not have to be repeated, and the effect would improve with every year.

May I thank all the kind people who have sent me helpful letters, pencils, and samples of labels? I now have a wonderful collection of every shape, size, colour, and substance. I am most grateful, and regret only that I have not been able to acknowledge each letter separately. Will those to whom I have not written, please accept my thanks in this way?

The most useful label comes from Messrs. G. J. Woodman, High Street, Pinner; strips of white plastic which you cut into lengths and fit into a metal holder.

October 14, 1951

As this month and the next bring round the time for planting shrubs, the ornamental quinces should not be forgotten. They may take a little while to get going, but, once they have made a start, they are there for ever, increasing in size and luxuriance from year to year. They need little attention, and will grow almost anywhere, in sun or shade. Although they are usually seen trained against a wall, notably on old farmhouses and cottages, it is not necessary to give them this protection, for they will do equally well grown as loose bushes in the open or in a border, and, indeed, it seems to me that their beauty is enhanced by this liberty offered to their arching sprays. Their fruits, which in autumn are as handsome as their flowers, make excellent jelly; in fact, there is everything to be said in favour of this well-mannered, easy-going, obliging and pleasantly old-fashioned plant.

The only grievance that people hold against it, for which the poor thing itself is scarcely to be blamed, is its frequent change of name. It started its career as *Pyrus Japonica*, and become familiarly known as Japonica, which simply means Japanese, and is thus as silly as calling a plant 'English' or 'French.' It then changed to Cydonia, meaning quince: *Cydonia japonica*, the Japanese quince. Now we are told to call it *chaenomeles*, but as I don't know what that means, beyond a vague idea that *chae* means hairy and *meles* means sombre or black, and as, furthermore, I am not at all sure how to pronounce it, I think I shall stick to Cydonia, which is in itself a pretty word. *

There are many varieties. There is the old red one, *C. lagenaria*, hard to surpass in richness of colour, beautiful against a grey wall or a whitewashed wall, horrible against modern red brick. There is *C. nivalis*, pure white, safely lovely against any background. There is *C. Moerloesii*, or the Apple-blossom quince, whose name is enough to suggest its shell-pink colouring. There is *Knaphill Scarlet*, not scarlet at all but coral-red; it goes on flowering at odd moments throughout the summer long after its true flowering season is done. There is *C. cathayensis*, with small flowers succeeded by the biggest green fruits you

* A correspondent rightly reproves me for ignorance and frivolity. *Chaenomeles*, he says, means 'Splitting Apple,' from the Greek *chaineis*, and *melea*, apple. Obviously, he is right, but I still don't like it.

ever saw—a sight in themselves. Finally, if you want a prostrate kind, there is *C. Simonii*, spreading horizontally, with dark red flowers, much to be recommended for a bank or a rock-garden.

Would Mr. J. Napier Proctor, who wrote to me asking for an address, please supply me with his own? Otherwise I shall be in his debt for life for 2½d., representing the stamp he so thoughtfully sent me.

October 21, 1951

The apples are ripening, and according to the old theory we shake them to hear if the pips rattle, or cut them in half to see if the pips have turned black. To how many of us has it occurred that those pips may be sown in a flower-pot, to be grown on into a little fruit-bearing tree for years to come? It might be a nice idea to sow some apple pips in commemoration of a birth or a christening, and to watch the growth of the infant tree keeping pace with the growth of the human infant. This is perhaps not a very serious form of gardening, but it is fun if you have the time to give to it. Nothing could be prettier than a small tree loaded with fruit. A correspondent tells me that after twelve years she picked a whole hundredweight of apples from a seedling she had raised herself; but then, admittedly, she had planted her seedling out: she had not kept it permanently in its pot.

All the same, it is possible to grow fruit trees in pots. Figs do very well. They fruit best when their roots are restricted, so the restriction of a pot is the very thing a fig needs, if it is not to run to leaf instead of to fruit. A pot-grown fig, heavily hung with its fruit among its beautifully shaped leaves, is a thing to stand on a paved path or beside a front door; it is decorative; and you can eat the figs. The hardy vines also make very good pot-plants. A fruiting vine, hung with bunches trained to arch round bamboo sticks stuck into a barrel sawn in half, is as pretty a sight as you could wish to see: it reminds one of some Italian paintings, and brings a suggestion of Mediterranean countries into our northern land. The hardy vines are not difficult to grow. I should plant the *Royal Muscadine*, with pale green-yellow grapes; or *Black Hamburgh*, which will do out-of-doors in our southern counties; or the Strawberry grape which I recommended in this column years ago, and which seems to have found favour with those enterprising gardeners who took my advice and acquired it. Its grey-pink bunches, hanging amongst the leaves, have a powdered look, as though they had been dusted over, delicately, with a puff.

Soft fruit can also be grown in pots. It is well known that strawberries can be made to pour out of a barrel pierced with holes all the way up; the small Alpine strawberry looks charming grown in this way. I remember also seeing a red currant, taught to grow as a little standard, about four feet high, with an umbrella-shaped head dripping with the tassels of its bright red beads. I see no reason why this idea should not be extended to the black and the white currants, and to gooseberries, or indeed to anything that will make a woody stem. Wineberries, loganberries, and raspberries would, of course, have to be trained round bamboo sticks, like the vines. There is great scope for inventiveness here; and the only recurrent care would be the renewal of the soil by an annual top-dressing, preferably of compost, to ensure that the plant with its limited root-run was not suffering from starvation. Also to see that it did not lack for water: plants in pots dry out very quickly.

October 28, 1951

If you are thinking of planting for autumn colouring, this is the time to look at the flaming shrubs and trees and to make your choice. In spring and summer one tends to forget the autumn days, but, when they arrive, with their melancholy and the spiders' webs so delicately and geometrically looped from the hedges, how grateful we are for the torch of a little tree or the low smoulder of leaves on azaleas and peonies. I feel sure that these effects should be concentrated into one area of the garden, preferably at a distance if space allows, so that they may be seen from the windows in a rabble incarnadine.

A visit to a local nursery will supply many suggestions. For my own part, I would plant a backing of the Cockspur thorn, *Crategus Crus galli*, and of the Scarlet Oak, *Quercus coccinea*, slow in growth but magnificently red in its October–November colour. If I had enough room, I would plant *Koelreuteria paniculata* behind these; it makes a tall tree in time; is seldom seen in our gardens; and contributes an astonishing pyramid of pink, yellow, and green at this time of the year. Then in front of all these I would plant *Prunus Sargentii*, a small tree pretty enough with its pink blossom in spring, but lovelier still in autumn when its leaves turn red, especially if you have planted it so that the early morning sun or the late afternoon sun can illuminate it and make the leaves transparent. This is a very important point, I think, which any gardener planting for autumn colour should observe: the transparency against the sun. I should then plant a whole host of autumn-colouring in front of these; little trees such as the peat-loving *Disanthus cercidifolium*, whose small round leaves dangle like golden coins; *Cornus kousa*; *Acer griseum*, *Nandina domestica*; *Euonymus alatus*, a most brilliant pink; *Rhus cotinoides foliis-purpureis*, the American sumach; and the low-growing, rounded bush of *Berberis Thunbergii*. As a ground covering for the front, there is a charming little bristly rose called *nitida*, which creeps about and forms a mat of blackish-red leaf and stem, not very showy from afar off perhaps, but pretty and unusual close to.

These are only a very few of the suggestions that could be made. I have not even mentioned the ornamental vines, such as *Coignettiae*, or the larger trees such as *Cercidiphyllum* or *Parrotia persica*. I might, however, refer you to Mr. Michael Haworth-Booth's new book, *Effective Flowering Shrubs* (Collins, 25s., with coloured photographs as illustrations), which is a reliable guide by that well-known authority.

I should like also to pay a tribute to Mr. George Russell, who has just died at the age of ninety-four. Starting as a garden boy at ten years old, he devoted many years of his life to the production of the strain we now know as the Russell lupins, with their remarkable range of colour, so far removed from the old monotonous blue. He must have been a dear old man. I never met him, but he used to write to me and send me his poems. I wish I could say that his poems were as good as his lupins.

October 5, 1952

The leaves are turning, and if there has been frost by the time this article appears, many of them will have been brought off. Their beauty, in some years, is evanescent, but if they hang only for a week it is supremely worth while to plant those trees or shrubs which, in their sudden blaze, will so startlingly recall the first glories of summer.

Among our native trees, the wild cherry or Gean is one of the first to turn. (I should perhaps qualify the word 'native' by saying that it may possibly have been introduced by the Romans, but after two thousand years its naturalization papers may surely be regarded as obsolete.) There is no need to emphasize the loveliness of the wild cherry in the spring, its great puffs of white appearing like the smoke of a train inexplicably stationary in the middle of bare woods. Its autumn colouring is no less sensational, but somehow one does not notice it so readily, because the

October leafage of the forest trees, oak, beech, and chestnut, still hangs so heavily green around it that it can be observed only close up or at a vista-cut of a distance.

Few people, alas, can afford to garden on so large a scale as to provide for long vista-cuts to-day. Those days of landscape gardening on the grand scale have gone, the days of Repton and Capability Brown, and the best hope now lies in the roadside planting carried out by local authorities. But we could still afford, modestly, to set our own wild cherry in a chosen place at the eastern or the western corner of the garden: I say eastern or western because the reddening leaves would then catch either the morning or the evening light, sunrise or sunset. Considering that it is a native, i.e. growing on its own roots without the labour of grafting, it is surprisingly expensive to buy from nurserymen, but energetic people living in the country can often find tall seedlings in the woods or hedgerows, or suckers springing up from the root in the neighbourhood of some mature specimen, and transplant them at no cost but an hour's labour. They can do so with the comforting reflection that their wildling has a life's anticipation of a century or more.

This is not written with any intention of encouraging people to despoil our countryside of its wild plants, but on the contrary with the intention of saving such wildlings as seem certain of an early doom at the hands of farmers or woodmen.

The Gean, or *Prunus avium*, is not to be confused with the Bird Cherry, in spite of its Latin name meaning 'of birds.' The Bird Cherry is *Prunus padus*, and is to be found growing wild in the north, rather than in the south, of Britain. There are also cultivated forms of the Bird Cherry: *P. padus Watereri* and *P. padus Albertii*. From personal acquaintance I can speak only of *P. padus Watereri*, which possesses what my nose tells me is a peculiarly honeyed scent.

October 12, 1952

A complaint commonly brought against many of the modern or 'improved' varieties of favourite old flowers is that they have lost their scent. In some cases this complaint is justified; in others not. The one which I want to consider in this article is the Sweet Pea, and it is quite an appropriate moment to do so, since this is the month when seeds may still be sown in pots for wintering in a frame and planting out next spring.

The true Sweet Pea, *Lathyrus odoratus*, small, hooded, and not remarkable for any beauty of colour, was originally sent from Italy in 1699 by a Father Cupani to Dr. Robert Uvedale, headmaster of the Grammar School at Enfield, Middlesex. Of Father Cupani I know nothing, but Dr. Uvedale, schoolmaster and horticulturist, seems to have been something of a character. He had a fine collection of foreign plants, which after his death in 1722 were sold to Sir Robert Walpole for his garden at Houghton in Norfolk. Of Dr. Uvedale it was said that 'his flowers were choice, his stock numerous, and his culture of them very methodical and curious.' Amongst them was the Sweet Pea, native of southern Italy and Sicily, and it is this which I should like to see restored to favour in this country.

Undoubtedly the Grandiflora and Spencer hybrids offer a greater range of colour, a greater solidity and length of stalk, and more flower-heads to a stalk, nor can it be said that they lack the fragrance which gives them their popular name. But compared with the fragrance of the humble little wildling they have nothing to boast about in that respect. It must be realized that the wild pea is not showy, in fact its pink and purple are very washy and the individual flowers are small, but they have a certain wistful delicacy of appearance and the scent of even half a dozen in a bunch is astonishing.

Unfortunately I cannot find them listed in any catalogue.

Even my favourite seedsman, who has over 3,000 numbers
to his credit and from whom one can buy the most improb-
able things, has failed me for once. This seems a depressingly
negative conclusion to come to, after so warm a recommendation, and I can suggest only that people with friends
in Italy (or Spain, where they also grow) should beg for
a packet of seed to be sent by post. Of course it is no good
attempting to grow them on the elaborate system of
training one stem up a bean-pole and suppressing all side
shoots; they must be left to scramble up twiggy pea-sticks
in a tangle and kept entirely for picking, in an unwanted
but sunny corner of the kitchen garden.

At the end of their season they can be left to set their
own seed and a supply be thus ensured. I know for a fact
that they do set and ripen their seed in this island, for I
have seen them doing it in a private garden quite far north,
and came away, I am glad to say, with a generous handful
which I hope to have growing in my own garden next
summer.

October 19, 1952

A word on the Burnet or Scots roses, so incredibly pretty,
mottled and marbled, self-coloured and two-coloured, and
moreover so easy to grow. As Mr. Edward Bunyard did not
fail to point out, there is no better covering for a dry bank,
since they will not only bind it together with their dense
root system, but will also run about underground and come
up everywhere in a little thorny jungle or thicket, keeping
the weeds away. They are also ideal plants for a poor starved
soil or for a windy place where taller, less tough things
might refuse to survive. Another of their virtues is that
they will make a charming low hedge. Their one drawback,
which one must admit to be serious, is that they flower only
once a year; but their foliage is quite pleasant to the eye,
and if they can be given a rough corner such as the dry

bank suggested by Mr. Bunyard, the brevity of their explosion in June may be forgiven them.

There is, however, an exception to this rule of short-lived flowering. *Stanwell perpetual* is its name. It is only half a Scot, being a hybrid between a Scot and a Damask, or possibly a Gallica; I like to think it has Gallica blood in it, since France and Scotland have always enjoyed a curious affinity as exemplified by their pepper-pot architecture and by certain phrases which have passed from one language into the other: *Ne vous fachez pas*, dinna fash yoursel'; and as for barley-sugar, or *sucre d'orge*, I could expand into a whole article over that.

This is by the way. The rose *Stanwell perpetual* is what I was writing about. I have become very fond of this modest rose, who truly merits the description *perpetual*. One is apt to overlook her during the great foison of early summer; but now in October, when every chosen flower is precious, I feel grateful to her for offering me her shell-pink, highly-scented, patiently-produced flowers, delicately doing her job again for my delectation in a glass on my table, and filling my room with such a good smell that it puffs at me as I open the door.

Stanwell perpetual grows taller than the average Scots rose. It grows four to five feet high. It is, as I have said, a hybrid. It has another name, according to Miss Nancy Lindsay, who is an expert on these old roses, the *Victorian Valentine rose*. This evokes pictures of old Valentines—but, however that may be, I do urge you to plant *Stanwell perpetual* in your garden to give you a reward of picking in October. Edwin Murrell, Ltd., has it, see p. 176.

October 26, 1952

A spike of the brightest orange caught my eye, half hidden by a clump of *Berberis Thunbergii* which had turned very much the same colour. They were both of an extraordinary brilliance in the low afternoon sunshine. I could not remember if I had planted them deliberately in juxtaposition, or if they had come together by a fortunate chance. Investigation revealed further spikes: three-sided seed-pods cracked wide open to expose the violent clusters of the berries within.

This was our native *Iris foetidissima* in its autumn dress, our only other native iris being the yellow waterside flag, *I. pseudo-acorus*. No one would plant *I. foetidissima* for the sake of its name, which in English is rendered the Stinking iris and derives from the unpleasant smell of the leaves if you bruise them. There is, however, no need to bruise leaves, a wanton pastime, and you can call it the Gladdon or Gladwyn iris if you prefer, or even the Roast-beef Plant. Some etymologists think that Gladdon or Gladwyn are corruptions of Gladiolus, owing to a similarity between the sword-like leaves; but I wish someone would tell me how it got its roast-beef name.

Its flowers, small, and of a dingy mauve, are of no value or charm, nor should we be wise to pick them, because it is for the seed pods that we cherish it. Not that it needs much cherishing, and is even one of those amiable plants that will tolerate shade. Strugglers with shady gardens, or with difficult shaded areas, will doubtless note this point. The seed-pods are for late autumn and winter decoration indoors, for the seeds have the unusual property of not dropping out when the pod bursts open, and will last for a long time in a vase; they look fine, and warm, under a table-lamp on a bleak evening. Miss Gertrude Jekyll used to advise hanging the bunch upside down for a bit, to stiffen the stalks; I dare say she was right; she was usually right, and had an experimental mind.

Let me not claim for the Gladdon iris that its crop of orange berries makes a subtle bunch or one which would appeal to flower-lovers of very delicate taste; it is frankly as coarse as it is showy, and has all the appearance of having been brought in by a pleased child after an afternoon's ramble through the copse. Nevertheless, its brightness is welcome, and its coarseness can be lightened by a few sprays of its companion the berberis. It can be bought at the low price of 1s. 6d. from the Orpington iris nursery, see p. 175 for address.

Taylor's Glory.

Page's Champion.

November

THE Master of the Worshipful Company of Gardeners recently wrote a letter to *The Times* expressing the hope that the pleasant occupation of window-box gardening might become a habit with our town-dwellers and might extend far beyond the special effort made during the Festival year. Judging by the number of letters I intermittently receive, urging me to write an article about town gardening in general and window-boxes in particular, I should say that his plea was likely to meet with a good response. The Worshipful Company three years ago gave two cups for an annual competition for City window-boxes, one for amateurs and one for professionals. They hope the competition will continue to receive support. Provincial cities might well imitate this happy idea; perhaps some of them do.

To my own *Observer* correspondents I have always been obliged to return the regretful answer that I had no experience of town gardening. Now, however, I have found the solution in an excellent little book called *Window-box and Indoor Gardening*, by Xenia Field (Collins, 10s. 6d.). You will realize from the title that this does not include *outdoor* gardens in cities; perhaps Xenia Field's publishers may persuade her to write one as a sequel, for I cannot imagine a better guide. She is knowledgeable, clear, practical to the point of being fool-proof, and full of ideas. She tells us all about how to make the window-box or boxes;

K

how to fill them with soil and drainage; what to plant in them; how to look after them; how to arrange for the seasonal flowers to succeed one another; giving admirably arranged lists of the take-it-or-leave-it type. 'These are my favourites,' she says in effect, 'but they may not be yours, so here I will give you an alternative choice.' Then, having finished with window-boxes filled with flowers, she comes on to window-boxes filled with herbs and salads; and then on to such varied things as Alpine gardens where 'Mountain peaks and ranges may be kept clean by wiping them over occasionally with soap and water, and if necessary a little Vim'; and then to gardens in miniature, and to plants to grow indoors, ending up with a chapter on nursery gardening, not the nursery of the nurseryman, but of the child, where bulbs may be grown in sponges, or grass in fir-cones, or acorns in eggshells, or a magic hyacinth may be created by spitting two bulbs in half, binding them together, and then growing the reconstructed bulb into a mongrel strange enough to stir the pride of any infant gardener exhibiting his trophy to his adult friends.

A nice, nice book; a useful book; a book to give for Christmas to all those flower-lovers who are condemned to live between bricks and stones; a book that will bring a touch of the country into the town.

November 11, 1951

A correspondent invites me to deal with a problem which he suggests must be confronting many people. He has, he says, a new house and a new garden in a new housing estate, and after three or four years his work will almost certainly compel him to move to another part of the country. What is he to do, (1) to secure privacy from his neighbours, and (2) to create some sort of a flower garden in the shortest possible time?

I am afraid the question does not offer much scope for

original suggestions. Impatience and gardening do not go well together. Still, something must be done. Privacy is the first essential, and privacy means a hedge. I do not much care for *Lonicera nitida*, which achieved so violent a popularity when it was first introduced some years ago, but there is no doubt that it is quick growing, dense, evergreen, and cheap at 90s. a hundred. The drawback is that it requires clipping so often if it is not to become straggly. Hornbeam is also quick-growing; a little more expensive at 120s. a hundred, it is not evergreen but does retain its crisp brown leaves throughout the winter so that it seldom looks quite bare. For a very rapid effect, *Polygonum baldschuanicum*, the Russian vine, with feathery white flowers in summer, is a good investment at 4s. 6d. each; not many plants would be needed to train along a fence, wires, or trellis. It is, however, deciduous, and would thus provide no true screen in winter. If this is not an absolute objection, a hedge made of fruiting brambles would be more unusual, also more remunerative; loganberries, wineberries, or the new Boysenberry, or the cultivated blackberry, especially the one called *Himalaya*, all of which can be bought for 4s. 6d. a plant. There would also be the rambler roses, so vigorous that within a year or two, given good feeding, the fence should be covered; there is no need to plant the old *Dorothy Perkins* or *American Pillar*, for far lovelier ones can be obtained at the same price, 4s. 6d. I should suggest *The New Dawn*, *Albertine*, *Félicité et Perpétue*, *Dr. Van Fleet*, *Albéric Barbier*, *François Juranville*.

As for the flower-garden I suppose quantities of hardy annuals must be the principal stand-by. This would involve making beds or borders with a reasonably good tilth of top-soil for seed-sowing. If my correspondent chooses beds, I trust he makes them sharply square or rectangular, and not in the shape of hearts, crescents, or lozenges. Of course, if he is prepared to go to the expense there is nothing to prevent him from filling them with some herbaceous perennials, flowering shrubs, or roses. Each man's problem must eventually be his own.

November 18, 1951

The family of the Sages is well known both in the kitchen-garden and the flower-garden. Some are aromatic herbs, scenting the hillsides in the sun of Mediterranean countries, and are associated in our minds with rough paths, goats, and olives. The sage is altogether an amiable plant; indeed, its Latin name, *Salvia*, comes from *salvere*, to save, or heal, and one of its nicknames is *S. salvatrix*, which sounds very reassuring. The common clary, or *S. sclarea*, is also known as Clear Eye and See Bright, not to be confused with Eyebright, that tiny annual whose proper name is Euphrasia. The French bestow a very genial personality on clary by calling it simply Toute Bonne, which to me at any rate suggests a rosy old countrywoman in a blue apron.

The kitchen sages make decorative clumps, for they can be had with reddish or variegated leaves as well as the ordinary grey-green. The garden sages are useful for the herbaceous border. I do not mean that half-hardy bedding-out plant beloved of the makers of public gardens, *S. splendens*, which should be forbidden by law to all but the most skilful handlers. I mean such old favourites as *S. virgata nemerosa*, a three-foot-high bushy grower whose blue-lipped flowers cluster amongst red-violet bracts and have the advantage of lasting a very long time in mid-summer; or *S. Grahami*, equally familiar, with durable red flowers, a Mexican, reasonably but not absolutely hardy. A more recent introduction, not yet so well known as it should be, is *S. haematodes*, greatly to be recommended; it grows about five feet high in a cloud of pale blue rising very happily behind any grey-foliaged plant such as the old English lavender. This salvia grows readily from seed, especially if sown as soon as it ripens, and will in fact produce dozens of seedlings of its own accord. It is good for picking, if you bruise the stems or dip their tips for a few moments into boiling water.

Anybody with the time to spare should grow *S. patens*. It is a nuisance in the same way as a dahlia is a nuisance, because its tubers have to be lifted in autumn, stored in a frost-proof place, started into growth under glass in April, and planted out again at the end of May. The reason for this is not so much the tenderness of the tubers themselves as the risk that a late frost will destroy the young shoots; possibly the use of a cloche or hand-light might obviate this danger. The amazing azure of the flowers, however, compensates for any extra trouble. Like the gentians, they rival the luminosity of the blue bits in a stained-glass window.

November 25, 1951

Perhaps few people share my taste for tattered-bark trees. I must concede that it is a special taste. I must concede also that unless you have a fairly large garden you cannot afford the space even for one or two specimens set aside in a neglected corner, to grow taller and taller as the years go on. So this must be an article for the few, not for the many.

I like the tattery trees, whose bark curls off in strips like shavings. There is one called *Arbutus Menziesii*, with cinnamon-red bark which starts to peel of its own accord, and which you can then smooth away with your hand into something like the touch of sand-papered wood of a curious olive-green colour. It likes a sheltered corner, for it is not absolutely hardy. Then there is *Acer griseum*, the Paper-bark maple, with mahogany-coloured bark replaced by a brighter orange underneath, and brilliantly red leaves in autumn. It is, in fact, one of the best for October–November colour. *Betula albo-sinensis var. septentrionalis* is a birch with a beautiful white-and-grey trunk; unfortunately I cannot find any nurseryman who now lists it, though I dare say inquiry might produce it.* It is, I think, one of the loveliest, though *Betula japonica* drips with most attractive little catkins in spring. This also appears to be unobtainable.

Prunus serrula, sometimes sold as *serrula tibetica*, is a very striking tree with a shiny mahogany bark. This does not take on so shaggy an appearance as some, but sheds its outer covering in circular strips, leaving the trunk with annular ridges that make it look as though it were wearing bracelets. Reddish and glossy, the freshly-revealed surface suggests the French polish sometimes used on fine old tables. It should be grown in very rich soil and planted where it can be seen, with the sun shining on it.

Now, having indulged myself by writing on a subject which I fear is not of very general interest, let me add a note on the Christmas roses or hellebores, which are just beginning to show their curly buds not unlike the first growth of young bracken. I have been told that the way to get long stems is to heap sand over the centre of the plant, when the flower-stalks, under the obligation of reaching for the light, will force their way upwards. I have never yet tried this method, but it seems common sense, and at the same time a glass cloche should be put right over the clump to prevent the flowers from getting splashed by rain and mud.

Everything is extraordinarily far forward this autumn; the winter jasmine is coming out rapidly, and the autumn-flowering cherry should be watched for its fat buds, which will open within a few days in the warmth of a room.

* Messrs. Hillier & Sons, Winchester, now list it at 15s. 6d.

Even the slugs are beginning to think about some precocious
buds of the Algerian iris.

November 2, 1952

I must depart for once from my usual practice of
recommending plants to grow in anybody's garden. The
fact is that I have got into trouble with my good friend
Mr. Jackman, of *Clematis Jackmanii* fame, and a very fine
nurseryman of shrubs and flowering trees to boot. Mr.
Jackman is angry with me for having told readers of these
articles to dig up wild cherries from the woods or hedgerows
where you get them for nothing except the time and labour
expended on finding them and digging them up.

I do see Mr. Jackman's point of view. It must be
infuriating for a nurseryman to read an article by an
amateur gardener such as I am, when he knows the financial
difficulties that he and his colleagues have to face. He
points out that a specimen tree nine to ten feet high costs
about 13s. 6d., and has taken fully five years to grow and
to train, and has had to be transplanted at least twice to
form a good root-system. You cannot just stick it in and
leave it to its own devices. Further, the minimum horticultural wage for a 50-hour week in 1939 was 35s. It is
now £5 12s. for 47 hours. There was then no statutory
holiday with pay; two weeks are now given. Other costs
beside wages have risen in proportion. Skilled work is still
necessary and always will be, since mechanization can play
but a relatively small part in the craft of gardening; yet
the average price of nursery stock is only two and a half
times pre-war price.

So far, I must endorse every argument that Mr. Jackman
puts forward. The financial facts are indisputable. There
is only one point in his letter which I would like to dispute,
and dispute most vigorously. He says that I use my column
to spread the idea that plants are surprisingly expensive

to buy from nurserymen and that I recommend 'gardening on the cheap.' The very last purpose for which I should wish to use my column is to spread the idea that nurserymen overcharge. They don't. And as for recommending gardening on the cheap, I should like on the contrary to encourage the most lavish extravagant planting everywhere, bulbs by the thousand instead of the hundred, flowering trees and shrubs by the hundred instead of by the dozen.

If Mr. Jackman were to read a cross-section of my correspondence, he would realize that, even as he is perfectly justified in stating the case for himself and his fellow-nurserymen, I, also, have a duty towards my more impecunious readers. Perhaps 60 per cent of my letters come from ardent gardeners whose desire for a bit of beauty is incommensurate with the dregs of their budget. Am I, therefore, to refrain from telling them to dig up a wild cherry, once in a way, when they can find one? And, in conclusion, if Mr. Jackman could see the replies, running now into thousands, which I have dispatched giving addresses of appropriate nurserymen, he might realize that, far from wishing to do harm to his most honourable profession, I have done my utmost to increase their order lists.

November 9, 1952

Although I missed the talk myself, I was glad to hear from a friend that one of the B.B.C. gardening experts, perhaps Mr. Streeter or Mr. Roy Hay, had spoken against the idea of red, white, and blue for Coronation-year planting. This combination of colour may be very much all right and heart-stirring for a flag, but it looks very discordant and unnatural in a garden. Patriotism, in this case, is not enough. We must look for something more permanent than the flag-like carpets of lobelia, alyssum, and scarlet salvia with which I fear our public and even our private gardens will be only too loyally patterned.

Not that I have anything against lobelia in itself. Properly used, in large pools, especially the sort called *Cambridge blue*, it can be regarded as a beautiful annual, rivalling my favourite *Phacelia campanularia*, blue as a gentian or the Mediterranean sea. Nor have I anything against Sweet Alyssum, smelling of honey in her lowly way. The thing I resent, on behalf of both these desirable plants, is that some bad godmother at their christening should have ordained a ribbon-development for them, an edging of bedding-out, where they have no space to expand into the big generous patches they deserve.

No. We must not be bound by thoughts of red, white, and blue in an effort to turn our gardens into temporary strips of bunting in 1953. We should concentrate rather on planting something more permanent: a young tree for a young Queen. A young tree that will grow with her reign until, as we hope, she attains the eventual age of her great-great-grandmother towards the year 2008; the sapling on which we expend half a guinea or as much more as we can afford to-day will by then have grown into a proud old tree, with a trunk and stout branches.

I might suggest planting a mulberry. It grows very quickly; it lives for hundreds of years; it produces fruit in a regular crop every summer; and it has a traditional historical character in this country. The fruit stains the hands, but Pliny tells us that the stain of the ripe berries can be cleaned off with the juice of unripe ones. I might also suggest planting a fig as a commemorative Coronation tree. Few people realize how well the fig will flourish in our southern counties, ripening its fruit as though in Italy. Naturally it does best against a wall, but there is at least one famous orchard, at Worthing, where it is grown as bushes in the open. A patriarchal bush in this orchard is said to date back to the days of Thomas à Becket, which speaks sufficiently well for its longevity.

November 16, 1952

In Tudor times, the Knot garden was fashionable. This meant a garden or parterre laid out on geometrical lines, with narrow paths between beds filled with flowers and outlined by little low hedges of some dwarf plant such as edging-box or cotton lavender, which would lend themselves to a neat clipping, or by certain clippable herbs such as the shrubby thymes, hyssop, and marjoram. An edging of thrift was also popular, and can be very pretty, both when it is in flower and when it is cushiony-green. The design of the knotted beds could be either simple or complicated; it could wriggle to any extent, as the word 'knot' clearly indicates; or it could be straight and severe, according to the taste of the owner. The flowers which filled the beds would necessarily be low-growing, not to over-top the little hedges; pansies and daisies come instantly to mind. If flowers were not wanted, the space could be filled in with tiny lawns of turf or camomile.

It occurred to me that the idea might well be adapted to present-day use. Even though we do not live in Tudor times, we do live in another Elizabethan age, and if we are thinking of Coronation planting we might well consecrate a separate area to the creation of such a garden. I think it should be flat, I mean level, though it need not be large; in fact the bit usually known as 'the front garden' would be eminently suitable and might be made to look very charming and unusual, as a change from the customary rose-beds or clumps of herbaceous plants. To vary the knots, it would be possible to plant the box or cotton lavender, or whatever you decide on, in the shape of initials, your own, your children's, or those of the Queen, an E.R. done in dwarf lavender for instance, closely trimmed, or in the dark green cushions of thrift which so soon join up and make a continuous lime. There is scope for ingenuity.

To turn to a different subject, may I put in a plea for the Home for aged gardeners at Horton in Buckinghamshire? It will accommodate thirty-five old gardeners and their wives, and in some special cases, their widows, and it wants donations, annual subscriptions, gifts in kind, endowments, legacies, or anything that we can spare. The old gardener who is past his work and who probably lost his tied cottage when he had to give up his job is a very appealing character. Adam, after all, was not only our first father but also our first gardener, and his descendant now comes cap in hand saying, 'Madam, I'm Adam,' in the same words as he may have used to introduce himself to Eve. You can read those words either way, forwards or backwards. Try.

A post card to the Secretary, Gardeners' Royal Benevolent Institution, 92 Victoria Street, London, S.W.1, will bring all particulars of the appeal that Adam is making.

November 23, 1952

How often I regret, as surely many amateur gardeners must regret, that I did not know more about the elementary principles of gardening when I first embarked on this enticing but tricky pastime. How many mistakes I could have avoided, and how far smaller could have been the coffer which my gardener now calls the Morgue, and which contains a multitude of metal labels representing the plants that have died on us over two decades of years. I suppose, however, that these remarks might apply to the whole of life—*si jeunesse savait*, and so on—and that one must go forward in the spirit of 'It's never too late to learn.'

One lesson that I have learnt is to plant things well from the start. A good start in life is as important to plants as it is to children: they must develop strong roots in a congenial soil, otherwise they will never make the growth that will serve them richly according to their needs in their adult life. It is important, it is indeed vital, to give a good start to any plant that you are now adding to your garden in this great planting month.

You may be planting some extra roses in this month of November, when roses are usually planted. Let me urge you to plant them with some peat and a handful of bone-meal mixed in with the peat. I did this last autumn on the recommendation of some rose-grower, I think it may have been Mr. Wheatcroft, and the effect on the root-growth of my experimental rose bushes was truly surprising to me when I dug them up this autumn to move them to another place. They had made a system of fibrous root such as I had never seen in so short a time. The reason is probably that peat retains moisture at the same time as giving good drainage, and that the bone meal supples nourishment.

It is usually supposed that roses enjoy a clay soil, and this I do believe to be true, having gardened in my early years on the stickiest clay to be found in the Weald of Kent. But what I now also believe to be true, is that although some plants such as roses will put up with a most disagreeable soil, they prefer to be treated in a more kindly fashion, having their bed prepared for them, dug out, and filled in with the type of soil they particularly favour. It is no use trying to grow the peat-lovers in an alkaline or chalky soil; everybody knows that, but what everybody does not realize is the enormous advantage to be gained from a thorough initial preparation. There should be no difficulty about that, in these days when nearly every gardener is his own compost-maker.

November 30, 1952

The Arbutus or Strawberry tree is not very often seen in these islands, except in south-west Eire, where it grows wild, but is an attractive evergreen of manageable size

and accommodating disposition. True, most varieties object
to lime, belonging as they do to the family of *ericaceae*,
like the heaths and the rhododendrons, but the one called
Arbutus unedo can safely be planted in any reasonable soil.

To enumerate its virtues. It is, as I have said, evergreen.
It will withstand sea-gales, being tough and woody. It has
an amusing, shaggy, reddish bark. It can be grown in the
open as a shrub, or trained against a wall, which perhaps
shows off the bark to its fullest advantage, especially if
you can place it where the setting sun will strike on it,
as on the trunk of a Scots pine. Its waxy, pinkish-white
flowers, hanging like clusters of tiny bells among the dark
green foliage, are useful for picking until the first frost
of November browns them; a drawback which can be
obviated by a hurried picking when frost threatens. And,
to my mind, its greatest charm is that it bears flower and
fruit at the same time, so that you get the strawberry-like
berries dangling red beneath the pale flowers. These berries
are edible, but I do not recommend them. According to
Pliny, who confused it with the real strawberry, the word
unedo, from *unum edo*, means 'I eat one,' thus indicating
that you don't come back for more.

After its virtues, its only fault: it is not quite hardy
enough for very cold districts, or for the North.

There is another arbutus called *Menziesii*, which is the
noble Madrona tree of California, reaching a height of
100 feet and more in its native home. I doubt if it would
ever reach that height in England, though I must admit
that the one I planted here in Kent some fifteen years
ago is growing with alarming rapidity and has already
obscured a ground-floor window; soon it will have attained
the next floor, and what do I do then? Let it grow as high
as the roof, I suppose, and beyond. Its lovely bark—
mahogany colour until it starts to peel, revealing an equally
lovely olive-green underneath—gives me such pleasure

that I could never bear to cut it down. Perhaps an exceptionally severe winter will deal with the problem, for it is marked with the dagger of warning, meaning 'tender' in the catalogues.

There is also *Arbutus Andrachne*, with the characteristic red bark, but this, again, is suitable only for favoured regions such as south and south-west England, parts of Wales, Northern Ireland, and south-west Eire. On the whole it is safer to stick to *Arbutus unedo*, so rewarding with its green leaves throughout the winter, and so pretty with its waxy racemes and scarlet fruits in autumn. It costs anything from 5s. 6d. to 10s. 6d., according to size, and is readily obtainable from most good nurserymen.

December

———

I HAVE often thought, and indeed have some recollection of having alluded to it in this column, that it would be amusing to devote a garden entirely to the native flora of the British Isles. Discrimination would be essential, and an avoidance of the stragglers and invaders, also some knowledge of the soil conditions necessary; for example, it would be absurd to plant heaths or other ericaceous subjects next to the chalk-lovers, or the inhabitants of marshy ground in the same patch as those tufts of thrift and sea-pink that blow so gaily and dryly from the crevices of our cliffs. But only an elementary recognition would be needed.

Let no impassioned preserver of our wild flowers imagine that I advocate a mischievous uprooting of rarities already threatened by the increase of arable land or by the depredations of well-meaning but ignorant amateur botanists. Over my dead body. . . . It is, however, possible (1) to collect seeds, (2) to buy specimens from a nurseryman, and furthermore some species might usefully be rescued from the danger of extermination. They might even benefit by being transplanted into better soil, and grow into finer plants, as the sky-blue chicory will.

It is impossible in so short an article to do more than indicate some kinds of wild flowers suitable for garden cultivation. Probably the first reaction of some people will be to exclaim 'Wild flowers? Do you mean weeds?' Think again. There are many which could not possibly be regarded as weeds. The fritillary, the small daffodil or Lent-lily, the lily of the valley, the yellow tulip *Sylvestris*, the autumn crocus, the claret-coloured *Daphne mezereum*, the several kinds of violet, purple or white, the green hellebore, the Gladwyn iris, the golden trollius, the marsh marigold, the Cheddar pink, Sweet Cicely, various campanulas, the water forget-me-not, the Burnet rose, some spurges, the snowdrop and the snowflake. This is leaving out of account the entire primrose family, also the orchids, which are most unlikely to survive transplantation. Buy them from a nursery if you must have them, but on no account dig them up.

We can produce only a humble little selection compared with the splendours of the Alps, the Dolomites, the Pyrenees, or Lebanon, but perhaps enough has been said to show that a botanical holiday might furnish at least a patch, hidden away from more sophisticated floral neighbours. It would have a reminiscent charm: 'Do you remember the day we came on the Welsh poppy?' 'I saw the Pasque-flower before you did.' It so happens that Mr. Walter Ingwersen has just brought out a book, *Wildflowers in the Garden* (Geoffrey Bles, 16s.), which is the ideal guide for anyone interested in this form of gardening; a book I had often wished for, and here it is.

December 9, 1951

It is pleasant to see the garden laid to bed for the winter. Brown blankets of earth cover the secret roots. Nothing is seen overground, but a lot is going on underneath in preparation for the spring. It is a good plan, I think, to leave a heavy mulch of fallen leaves over the flowering shrubs instead of sweeping them all away. They serve the double purpose of providing protection against frost, and of eventually rotting down into the valuable humus that all plants need. There are leaves and leaves, of course, and not all of them will rot as quickly as others. Oak and beech are the best, to compose into leaf mould in a large square pile; but any leaves will serve as a mulch over beds and borders throughout the hard months to come.

The professional gardener will raise objections. He will tell you that the leaves will 'blow all over the place' as soon as a wind gets up. This is true up to a point, but can be prevented by a light scattering of soil or sand over the leaves to hold them down. This sort of objection may often be overcome by the application of some common sense. There are few people more obstinate than the professional or jobbing gardener. Stuck in his ideas, he won't budge.

November and December make a difficult blank time for the gardener. One has to fall back on the berrying plants; and amongst these I would like to recommend the seldom-grown *Celastrus orbiculatus*. This is a rampant climber, which will writhe itself up into any old valueless fruit tree, apple or pear, or over the roof of a shed, or over any space not wanted for anything more choice. It is rather a dull green plant during the summer months; you would not notice it then at all; but in the autumn months of October and November it produces its butter-yellow berries which presently break open to show the orange seeds, garish as heraldry, *gules* and *or*, startling to pick for indoors when set in trails against dark wood panelling, but equally lovely against a white-painted wall.

It is a twisting thing. It wriggles itself into corkscrews, not to be disentangled, but this does not matter because it never needs pruning unless you want to keep it under control. My only need has been to haul it down from a tree into which it was growing too vigorously; a young prunus, which would soon have been smothered. Planted at the foot of an old dead or dying tree, it can be left to find its way upwards and hang down in beaded swags, rich

L

for indoor picking, like thousands of tiny Hunter's moons coming up over the eastern horizon on a frosty night.

December 16, 1951

An article I wrote some weeks ago about growing strawberries in tubs or barrels seems to have aroused interest in readers of *The Observer*. I did think it was a good idea for people who have a limited area of garden. You waste no ground space, and you set your tubs anywhere you want them, either side of the front door or sideways along the garden path. It now occurs to me that the idea could be extended to alpines or other small plants, grown in the same way in barrels sawn in half round their equator.

Why not? It is an easy idea to carry out. You buy your barrel from a local sale; put a thick layer of crocks all over the bottom, not forgetting to pierce a hole or holes for drainage first; you then fill it with soil and plant your treasures. The kind of soil you fill it with will depend upon what kind of treasures you wish to grow. Alpines, generally speaking, like a somewhat gritty soil which will afford them the good, open drainage that prevents them from rotting off. Stagnant damp is a far greater enemy than frost or drought in this country. A gritty soil may be achieved by mixing a barrow-full of fibrous loam, taken from the top-spit of an old meadow, with some sharp sand and a generous helping of stone chippings such as one sees piled in such enticing heaps by the roadside. It is unfortunate that these should be the property of the county council. Were I not inherently honest (or, perhaps, cowardly), I should be sorely tempted to go out with a shovel and barrow at dead of night.

Flat-growing subjects such as saxifrages would probably be best for a groundwork on top, making squabs of silvery grey, something like a round Victorian pincushion, breaking out into their tiny rosy flowers in the spring. The sorts called *Irvingii, Cranbourne, Jenkinsonii,* are all very small, tight, and pretty. But you can be more ambitious with your barrel if you want to plant other things half way up it. You can plant things which like pouring out sideways, making miniature waterfalls of flower, little Niagaras of foam in the saxifrage called *Tumbling Waters*—twelve inches long in its flower tassel, hanging down, very handsome and yet very delicate. Another plant I would like to set into the sideway holes of the sawn barrel is *Lewisia.* The *Lewisias* are not too easy-going, which is perhaps the reason they are so seldom seen; but they are certainly plants for any gardener prepared to accept a challenge. They make rosettes of leaf, and throw out sprays of chintz-like flowers, pink or creamy, very elegant and old-fashioned looking. They should do well planted sideways in the barrel, on the principle that they are very happy growing out of a dry wall; it should be remembered, however, that they dislike lime. They also dislike disturbance, and the best way to propagate them is by seed.

December 23, 1951

As this article will appear two days before Christmas, I thought I would write on the most unsuitable unseasonable subject I could think of: roses. We may be under snow by then, and the very thought of a rose will be warming. Besides, roses can still be planted any time between December and March, so it is not too late to order extravagantly on any plant-token you may receive as a Christmas present.

There are roses and roses. My own taste in roses is perhaps not everybody's taste, and I am afraid that I may too often have tried to force it upon readers of *The Observer.* I know that I tend always towards the species roses, and the great wild shrubby roses flinging themselves about,

L*

instead of those neat little, hard little, tight little scrimpy dwarfs we call the hybrid teas.

On the subject of hybrid teas I have never quite made up my mind. I am torn. I see their beauty. I see their usefulness. I see that you can pick them all through the summer right up into the late autumn. You can fill a bowl with them even into December when, strangely enough, they sometimes throw a more richly coloured and more richly scented bloom. Yet for some reason they do not catch my heart. I have, however, succumbed at last and planted a dozen, purely for picking, in a corner of the kitchen garden. The chosen ones were *Ena Harkness, Ophelia, Etoile de Hollande, Charles Mallerin, Christopher Stone, Lady Sylvia, Mrs. Van Rossem, Emma Wright, Crimson Glory, Mrs. Sam McGredy, The Doctor, McGredy's Sunset.* I hope they will not all develop black spot, but I expect they will.

There are several schools of thought on the control of this worry, which causes complete defoliation in bad cases and must end in destroying the constitution of the plant, thus deprived of its natural means of breathing through the leaves. The orthodox method is spraying with Bordeaux mixture in January and February. T.M.T., or Thiram, sometimes supplied under the name *Tulisan,* is also recommended for fortnightly use from the end of May onwards. Some rose-growers also advise a thick mulch of lawn clippings, peat-moss litter, or even sawdust. Others put their faith (such as it is) in rich feeding, on the principle that a healthy, well-nourished plant is more resistant to infection. I must say that I found this works well. It may sound unscientific, since black spot is a fungus, and you might imagine that a fungus would establish itself on weak or strong plants equally once it had made up its mind to do so; but I am not a scientific gardener and can judge only by results. The result of some barrow-loads of compost was: no black spot on some particularly vulnerable roses two summers running, including the damp summer we have recently disenjoyed.

I would like to mention here a useful new book called *The Rose in Britain*, by N. P. Harvey, published by Plant Protection, Ltd., 17s. 6d., with many illustrations in colour.

December 30, 1951

Nearly the New Year. I know someone who averts his eyes from all young growth, such as narcissus leaves pushing through, prior to January 1st, but who, after that date, peers eagerly in the hope of even a rathe snowdrop. We know full well that January and February can be the most unpleasant months in the calendar, but they do bring some consolation in the beginnings of revival. Crocuses and other small bulbs appear, miraculous and welcome; they are apt, however, to leave a blank after they have died down, and it is for that reason that I suggest overplanting them with some little shrubs which will flower in February or March.

I visualize a low bank or slope of ground, not necessarily more than two or three feet high, perhaps bordering some rough steps on a curve. You stuff and cram the bank with early-flowering bulbs, making a gay chintzlike or porcelain effect with their bright colours in yellow, blue, white, orange, red. Amongst these, you plant the little shrubs I want to recommend, *Corylopsis spicata* and *Corylopsis paucifolia* are two of the prettiest and softest, hung with yellow moths of flowers all along their twiggy branches. They are natives of Japan, and are related to the witch-hazels. They seldom grow more than four feet high and about as much through; they need no pruning, and are graceful in their growth, pale as a primrose, and as early. Another little companion shrub on the bank would be *Forsythia ovata*. The big bushy forsythia is well known, but this small relation from Korea is not so often seen. It is perfectly hardy, and makes a tiny tree three to four feet high, flowering into the familiar golden blossoms, a golden rain pouring down in companionship with the *Corylopsis*, after the bulbs have died away.

There is also a dwarf variety of the favourite *Viburnum fragrans*, called *compactum*, which would associate happily.

If you have room in your garden at the top of the bank or slope, I would urge you to plant *Cornus mas*, the Cornelian cherry. This cornel or dog-wood produces its yellow flowers in February, and is one of the best winter flowerers for picking for indoors. A big full-grown tree of *Cornus mas* is a sight to be seen, as I once saw one growing in a wood in Kent. It towered up fifteen feet and more, smothered in its myriads of tiny clusters, each individual flower-head like a bunch of snipped ribbons. If at first it seems a little disappointing and makes only a thin show, do not be discouraged, for it improves yearly with age and size, and one year will suddenly surprise you by the wealth of its blossom. It also produces long scarlet berries which you can, if you wish, eat.

December 7, 1952

Christmas presents for gardening friends? People living in towns will presumably be reduced to visiting the nearest florist and will come away with a pot of Persian cyclamen, confident that, if properly treated, it will continue to give pleasure for years. May I point out to them that very occasionally you find a *scented* cyclamen? It is worth sniffing round the array in the hope of coming across one with this additional charm.

If, however, you want to give something rather less obvious than a ready-made plant in a pot, why not compose a miniature garden in what is known to horticultural sundriesmen as an Alpine pan? You can furnish this for

yourself with suitable small subjects which can be ordered
for about 1s. 6d. each from any appropriate nurseryman,
and can safely be planted now or at any time, since they
are supplied ex-pots. The *sedums* or Stone-crops, and the
Sempervivums or house-leeks, are all useful for this purpose,
being to all intents and purposes indestructible; but there
are lovelier things such as the Saxifrages, and the little
pink daisies, *Bellis Dresden China*, and the minute blue
forget-me-not, *Myosotis rupicola*, which make a pretty
group, not flowering in time for Christmas, but a delight
to watch for, long after most Christmas presents have been
absorbed into daily life.

Ingenuity and imagination can make a very pretty
thing out of an Alpine pan. For instance, a few flat stones
laid between the plants to divide them, stones an inch
or so in width or length; or bulkier stones stuck upright
like tiny Dolomites.

Other suggestions. For the country friend: plant-tokens,
now available from most nurserymen and seedsmen as
book-tokens are available from booksellers, enabling him
or her to choose what he or she wants, instead of ordering
something which may turn out to be more of a white
elephant than a pleasure. Fertilizers such as bone-meal or
hop-manure. Or a bale of Somerset or Cumberland peat.
Tools: these are always useful, because tools wear out and
have to be replaced. John Innes compost, for seed boxes
and many other uses. String, in tarred balls or in spools
of green twist. Secateurs, to carry in the pocket. Knives,
pruning, budding, or just a big sharp knife. And finally,
for your own children or for your nephews and nieces, a
cactus—because they couldn't kill it even if they tried.

December 14, 1952

May I remind readers about the winter-flowering cherry,
Prunus subhirtella autumnalis? I know I have mentioned

it before, but that was a long time ago, and as the seasons come round one remembers the things one tends in one's ingratitude to forget during the rich months of spring and summer; besides, there are the Christmas plant-tokens to think of. This cherry was in full flower in the open during the first fortnight of November; I picked bucketfuls of the long, white sprays; then came two nights of frost on November 15th and 16th; the remaining blossom was very literally browned-off; I despaired of getting any more for weeks to come. But ten days later, when the weather had more or less recovered itself, a whole new batch of buds was ready to come out, and I got another bucketful as fresh and white and virgin as anything in May.

There is a variety of this cherry called *rosea*, slightly tinged with pink; I prefer the pure white myself, but that is a matter of taste. There is also another winter-flowering cherry, *Prunus serrulata Fudanzakura*, which I confess I neither grow nor know, and I don't like recommending plants of which I have no personal experience, but the advice of Captain Collingwood Ingram, the 'Cherry' Ingram of Japanese cherry fame, is good enough for me and should be good enough for anybody. This, again, is a white single-flowered blossom with a pink bud, and may be admired out of doors or picked for indoors any time between November and April. So obliging a visitor from the Far East is surely to be welcomed to our gardens.

By the way, I suppose all those who like to have some flowers in their rooms even during the bleakest months are familiar with the hint of putting the cut branches, such as the winter-flowering cherry, into almost boiling hot water? It makes them, in the common phrase, 'jump to it.'

Have I ever mentioned, amongst early flowering shrubs, *Corylopsis paucifolia*? I believe I have, but it will do no harm to put in a reminder. The Corylopsis is a little shrub, not

more than four or five feet high and about the same in
width, gracefully hung with pale yellow flowers along the
leafless twigs, March to April, a darling of prettiness.
Corylopsis spicata is much the same, but grows rather
taller, up to six feet, and is, if anything, more frost-
resistant. They are not particular as to soil, but they do
like a sheltered position, if you can give it them, say with
a backing of other wind-breaking shrubs against the
prevailing wind.

Sparrows. . . . They peck the buds off, so put a bit of
old fruit-netting over the plant in October or November
when the buds are forming. Sparrows are doing the same
to my Winter-Sweet this year, as never before; sheer
mischief; an avian form of juvenile delinquency; so take the
hint and protect the buds with netting before it is too late.

December 21, 1952

Christmas approaches, and perhaps I ought to be writing
about mistletoe and holly, but I would rather go back to
summer and try to revive some of its warm pleasures. We
had the nastiest month of November, when the weather
did everything it could think of: frost, snow, rain, floods,
gales; but, even through that disagreeable span, one little
climber persisted in flowering and I would like to record
my gratitude. It had started flowering from early May
onwards, and by December 1st it was still in flower.

This was *Abutilon megapotamicum*. Its apparently
alarming name means merely an Arabic word associated
with the Mallows, a botanical family to which our familiar
garden hollyhocks belong; and *megapotamicum*, the great
river, meaning the Amazon in Brazil.

Abutilon megapotamicum bears no resemblance at all to
the hollyhocks as we know them in cottage gardens. It
is a thing to train up against a sunny south wall, and if
you should happen to have a whitewashed wall or even

a wall of gray stone, it will show up to special advantage against it. It has long pointed leaves and a curiously shaped flower, dark red and yellow, somewhat like a fuchsia, hanging from flexible, limp, graceful sprays. It is on the tender side, not liking too many degrees of frost, so should be covered over in winter. But perhaps you know all this already.

The idea I wanted to put forward is something that occurred to me accidentally, as gardening ideas do sometimes occur to one. I thought how pretty it might be to train an Abutilon as a standard. You see, it could be persuaded to weep downwards, like a weeping willow or a weeping cherry, if you grew it up on a short stem and constantly trimmed off all the side shoots it tried to make, till you got a big rounded head pouring downwards like a fountain dripping with the red and yellow flowers for months and months and months throughout the summer.

Is that a good idea? I have not tried it yet, but I intend to. Of course, for anyone who has the advantage of a greenhouse, however small and unheated, a little standard of an Abutilon in a big flower-pot might remain in flower well into the winter, and could be carried indoors for Christmas.

December 28, 1952

This seems a good occasion to mention the Christmas rose, *Helleborus niger*, in high Dutch called Christ's herb, 'because it flowereth about the birth of our Lord.' Its white flowers are, or should be, already on our tables. There is a variety called *altifolius*, which is considered superior, owing to its longer stalks; but it is often stained with a somewhat dirty pink, and I think the pure white is far lovelier. Christmas roses like a rather moist, semi-shady place in rich soil, though they have no objection to lime; they do not relish disturbance, but if you decide to plant some clumps you should do so as soon as they have finished flowering, which is another good reason for mentioning them now. If you already have old-established clumps, feed them well in February with a top dressing of compost or rotted manure, or even a watering of liquid manure, and never let them get too dry in summer. It is perhaps superfluous to say that they should be protected by a cloche when the buds begin to open, not because they are not hardy but because the low-growing flowers get splashed and spoilt by rain and bouncing mud.

The Christmas rose, although not a native of Britain, has been for centuries in our gardens. Spenser refers to it in the *Faerie Queene*, and it is described as early as 1597 in his *Herball* by John Gerard, who considered that a purgation of hellebore was 'good for mad and furious men.' Such a decoction might still come in useful to-day. Perhaps Gerard was quoting Epictetus, who, writing in the first century A.D., remarks that the more firmly deluded is a madman, the more hellebore he needs. Unfortunately, this serviceable plant is not very cheap to buy, costing anything from 5s. 6d. to 7s. 6d., but on the other hand it is a very good investment because, to my positive knowledge, it will endure and even increase in strength for fifty years and more. It is also possible, and not difficult, to grow it from seed, but if you want to do that you should make sure of getting freshly ripened seed, otherwise you may despair of germination after twelve months have gone by and will crossly throw away a pan of perfectly viable seeds which only demanded a little more patience.

I have a great affection for all the hellebores, and would like to return to the subject, with especial reference to our own two native kinds, *H. viridis* and *H. foetidus*. (See pp. 21–22.)